RETURN TO ME

Joseph Pollard

Return to Me

REFLECTIONS FOR EACH DAY OF LENT

the columba press

First published in 2005 by
the columba press
55A Spruce Avenue, Stillorgan Industrial Park,
Blackrock, Co Dublin

Cover by Bill Bolger
Origination by The Columba Press
Printed in Ireland by ColourBooks Ltd, Dublin

ISBN 1 85607 531 1

Acknowledgements
Scripture quotations are taken from the New Revised Standard Version
Bible, copyright (c) 1989 by the Division of Christian Education of the
National Council of the Churches of Christ in the USA, and are used by
permission.

Table of Contents

Introduction	7
Return to Me!	8
Costly Grace	10
True Fasting	12
Removing Affliction	15
Blessed Disruption	17
The Call to be Holy	19
Potent Words	21
Attend to the Lord!	23
The Golden Rule	25
The Spirit of Religion	27
Stretching Our Love	29
Are You Saved?	31
Sin as Treachery	33
True Repentance	35
Patterns of Leadership	37
True Wisdom	39
New Tenants	41
Shepherding	43
Cleaning House	45
Facing Rejection	48

No Frontiers   50

Lessening Our Losses   52

About Neutrality   54

Conversion   56

An Offer Refused   58

Lifted Up For Us   60

From a Distance   62

Healing Us   64

Declaring His Authority   66

The Crucial Voice   68

Remaining Righteous   70

Amazing Grace   72

The Hour   74

Not Judging Others   77

Going His Way   79

Truth and Freedom   81

Keep His Word!   83

Refusing to Give Way   85

Blessed Expediency   87

The Saviour of Israel   89

Anointing For Burial   92

Following Him   94

Never Despairing   96

Service Always   98

Were You There?   100

Seeing Deeper Than Sight   103

Introduction

In his book, *A Cry for Mercy*, Henri Nouwen asks if we can really celebrate Easter without observing Lent. Can we rejoice in the resurrection if we do not share in the passion and death of our Lord?

Our celebration of Lent has to have something of suffering and death to it. There is pain involved in breaking bad habits; there is effort involved in acquiring good ones. We may have to let go of some comfort which has become uncomfortable to the work of the Spirit within. We may have to pull down defences that only keep God and neighbour at a distance. Therefore we could call Lent a season of small deaths as we disengage on one level and engage on another. It is the season of restoration and renewal in our lives.

St Paul makes an observation which may help propel our efforts, and which gets to the spiritual heart of Lent. He says, 'While we live we are always being given up to death for Jesus' sake, so that the life of Jesus may be made visible in our mortal flesh.' (2 Cor 4:11) Christian penance always has this sublime purpose.

The scripture passages for reflection in this book are used in the liturgy of the weekdays and Sundays of Lent. Reflections for the days of the Sacred Triduum are included. Each reflection concludes with a prayer. An activity is suggested for each week of Lent.

Ash Wednesday

Return to Me!

Scripture passage

> Yet even now, says the Lord,
> return to me with all your heart,
> with fasting, with weeping, and with mourning;
> rend your hearts and not your clothing.
> Return to the Lord, your God,
> for he is gracious and merciful,
> slow to anger, and abounding in steadfast love,
> and relents from punishing.
> (Joel 2: 12-13)

Reflection

The church uses the prophet Joel's call to repentance to open the Lenten season. Joel lived roughly four centuries before Christ. His calling of God's people to repentance was occasioned by a plague of locusts and a drought which struck the land. These two phenomena often went hand-in-hand to create famine. Indeed, they still do in various parts of our world as we see in the news reports on our TV screens.

Joel interprets the invasion of the locusts as a punishment of God for sin. So he issues the call to repentance. If repentance is undergone, God will not only relent but may even return his people to their exclusive relationship with him. However, the repentance which Joel calls for, on behalf of God, is repentance in depth and with feeling: 'Return to me with all your heart.'

Joel's words, while addressing all God's chosen people, are particularly focused on the Jerusalem community of which Joel himself is a member. He wants repentance from the Jerusalem community and from every strand of it including its temple priests. Joel is probably a temple priest himself.

Joel's call to repentance reaches across the centuries to ourselves now as we begin our Lent. Many of us have little difficulty in recognising our sinfulness and our need of repentance. We know that we are always falling a bit short of the mark. But others of us – perhaps especially those in the so-called professions – may be so used to our positions of leadership, of presiding, of teaching others and lifting up the wounded and re-directing the wayward that we do not notice our own weaknesses and wounds and our need of repentance. Lent is a good time to pause and to take stock.

Prayer
Heavenly Father: Grant me a repentant heart. There is much in my life's history calling for repentance. And there is much in my present-day living that is marked by sin and other signs of a less than fully committed heart. May I ask for the grace of being whole-hearted in my repentance so that I may journey through Lent to Easter in solidarity with your self-sacrificing Son? May your grace impel me to rend my heart and not my clothing, as Joel puts it. May I return to you with all my heart. Amen.

Activity for the rest of this week
The ashes are placed on my forehead today with the exhortation, 'Repent, and believe in the gospel!' The ashes wear off but not the exhortation! I will make a greater effort each day this week to live the gospel as my rule of life. May all I meet find the gospel witnessed in my words and actions.

Thursday after Ash Wednesday

Costly Grace

Scripture passage

>[Jesus said to his disciples], 'The Son of Man must undergo
>great suffering, and be rejected by the elders, chief priests,
>and scribes, and be killed, and on the third day be raised.'
>Then he said to them all, 'If any want to become my follow-
>ers, let them deny themselves and take up their cross daily
>and follow me. For those who want to save their life will lose
>it, and those who lose their life for my sake will save it. What
>does it profit them if they gain the whole world, but lose or
>forfeit themselves?'
>(Lk. 9: 22-25)

Reflection

The German pastor Dietrich Bonhoeffer, who was executed by
the Nazis, wrote about 'cheap' and 'costly' grace. He wanted
Christians to appreciate the fact that God's graciousness in their
regard, his forgiveness and his love, come at a price. They come
at the price of the passion and death of his beloved Son. Grace is
not cheap grace then: it is very costly grace.

As a consequence, no one should assume that the road to
sanctity or to heaven is an easy one, or that being a real Christian
is a stroll in the park. There can be no 'comfortable Christians.'
Jesus' own words in our scripture passage are forthright. He
says that for grace and salvation in our lives, he must undergo
'great suffering' and 'be killed'.

Our grace and salvation were not cheaply bought and following the Lord is not an inexpensive effort. It is costly. 'If any
want to become my followers, let them deny themselves and
take up their cross daily and follow me.' Our Lord wants genuine followers. He wants true disciples. He does not want fair
weather friends who have no real loyalty or commitment. On
the other hand, he doesn't expect those who choose to follow
him to be ready-made mystics and already polished saints. He

calls ordinary people of good heart to follow him in the way of the kingdom of God. It's a long road and it takes – exactly – the length of our lives.

The cross we are asked to carry, in imitation of Jesus, requires us to shoulder cheerfully the challenges of our calling in life and the ups and downs of the day. It requires us to bear the burden of criticism or antagonism which we may encounter because of our loyalty to Christ and his standards. It requires us to spend much of our time and energy on others' needs rather than our own. For those of us who have chosen to follow Jesus and to take up the cross, there is encouragement in his observation that people who live for this world and for themselves will lose their world and their lives in the long run, whereas those who invest their lives in following him and in serving others will arrive in eternal life.

Prayer

Lord Jesus: Help me to accept the cross in my life and to bear it willingly as you bore yours for me. Help me whether the cross is just the boredom of the day or the unexpected death of a family member. Help me when the cross is an addiction in my family or violence in the neighbourhood. Help me bear my cross when it is the sad remembrance of past opportunities missed, of roads not taken, and graces ignored. Help me if the cross enters my life as a major illness and, all the more, if it enters as a terminal one. Look kindly on me and on my crosses even as you remember the awful burden of your own. Thank you. Amen.

Friday after Ash Wednesday

True Fasting

Scripture passage
> Is not this the fast that I choose:
> to loose the bonds of injustice,
> to undo the thongs of the yoke,
> to let the oppressed go free,
> and to break every yoke?
> Is it not to share your bread with the hungry,
> and to bring the homeless poor into your house;
> when you see the naked, to cover them,
> and not to hide yourself from your own kin?
> (Isa 58: 6-7)

Reflection
In this passage God answers his chosen people's question, 'Why do we fast, but you do not see?' (Isa 58: 3) God's answer is that his people do the wrong kind of fasting. And they do it for selfish reasons. God tells them the kind of fasting he desires in our scripture passage.

The first thing we can say about the kind of fasting God desires – according to this scripture – is that it has little to do with the traditional 'giving up things for Lent' such as sweets, smokes, a bet or two on the nags, and glorious Guinness! Nor is true fasting the call to ritual, such as temple worship then or going to Mass for Lent now. This is not to say that such practices do not entail a measure of fast and penance but they are not the fasting which God names. The fasting God names is working for social justice and harmony in human relationships. True fasting is about setting things right. It's about undoing social wrongs, righting imbalances, cutting people some slack when they need it, and harmony in one's own household and 'among your own kin'.

God wants our time and effort spent in righting social wrongs. We are challenged to 'loose the bonds of injustice' and to 'break every yoke' that keeps human beings from being free and full persons. In practical terms this means that if I employ someone I must be a just employer; if I am an employee I must do a decent day's work. An exploited worker is not served by the sweets or the smokes that I, as employer, give up for Lent. He or she is served only by the justice I owe them. Similarly, the neglect of patients in my nursing home is not absolved by my going to Mass every day in Lent, but by the caring service I owe them as a matter of justice.

God also desires the form of fasting that involves charity. Do I share my bread with the hungry, care for the homeless, and clothe the naked? These, and similar actions of kindness, form what were called the corporal works of mercy. They were a great concern of Jesus' heart and teaching. (cf Mt 25:31-40) Hunger, homelessness and want confront us these days on a huge scale and especially on the international level. Our kindness, therefore, is often best channelled through the relief agencies and the NGOs that are active on the international level, and through proven organisations such as the St. Vincent de Paul Society at the local level.

And God desires that we 'Do not hide yourself from your own kin.' What does God mean? Briefly, he wants us to commit to harmonious relationships in family life. The harmonisation of relationships is a form of true fasting because it is no easy task, and much has to be invested by way of time and energy as family members move through the stages and stresses of finding their feet, growing up, moving on, and growing old. The passing of the years only adds to the size of the extended family and increases the range and the burden of harmonisation. It is one form of fasting and penance that is always with us.

Prayer
Heavenly Father: Help me to fast as you desire your holy people to fast. May my fast be the spending of my time and energy on matters of justice, charity and harmony. May my fast be the discipline of one who is scrupulously just in his and her dealings

and relationships. Let my fast be my generosity in the face of hunger and the many forms of human impoverishment. Let my fast be my dedication to peace-making in my own home and my support of harmonious relationships in the extended family, the parish and the community. I ask your encouragement as I fast in this manner in the name of Jesus, your Son, and through the inspiration and the impulses of your Holy Spirit. Amen.

Saturday after Ash Wednesday

Removing Affliction

Scripture passage

> If you remove the yoke from among you,
> false accusation and malicious speech,
> if you offer your food to the hungry
> and satisfy the needs of the afflicted,
> then your light shall rise in the darkness
> and your gloom be like the noonday ...
> Your ancient ruins shall be rebuilt;
> you shall raise up the foundations of many generations;
> you shall be called the repairer of the breach,
> the restorer of streets to live in.
> (Isa 58:9-10, 12)

Reflection

Our scripture passage is a continuation of yesterday's scripture passage. The subject is still the nature of true fasting, or the kind of fasting God desires us to engage in. True fasting is a matter of the good heart and the effort required in serving the interests of justice and kindness.

The 'yoke' which God wants us to 'remove from among you' is the yoke of affliction. Affliction has many forms. It is injustice, poverty, hunger, disharmony at home and in human relationships. These were named in yesterday's scripture passage. We could add many more simply with reference to the various lists of human and civil rights that have emerged since the UN Declaration of Human Rights in 1948.

Our scripture passage today names false accusation and malicious speech as afflictions to be removed from our midst. We should not inflict these welts on others. False accusation and malicious speech (or gossip) are often condemned in the Old Testament and mainly because they ill-become the people God calls his own. In addition, they create disturbance among people and can lead to splits in the community. There is often considerable fasting involved in just keeping our mouth shut, so to speak, since we all love to gossip and are prone to embellish.

We do well to accept God's word, spoken through Isaiah, that the fasting he wants from us relates to issues of justice and to expressions of kindness. In God's frame of reference, Lenten fasting is not about giving up sweets but about giving up a narrow social vision and untying the strings of a taut heart. As the biblical scholar John J. Collins puts it, 'Isaiah anticipates the criteria for the final judgement [given by Jesus in Mt 25:31-46] ... and is drawing on a long tradition of prophetic criticism which insists that worship without justice has no value.' (*Collegeville Bible Commentary*)

If we fast after the manner of God's desire, we please him and we put in place what our scripture passage calls 'the foundations of many generations' to come. Justice and kindness, commitment to fairness and decency, help to restore 'the ruins' in religious life and in social life. Thus we help build the kingdom and the future. And our pursuit of justice and our display of kindness allow us to be called 'the repairers of the breach' between God and man, and to be named 'the restorers of the streets' of the community or city in which we live.

Prayer
Heavenly Father: Help me to fast in line with your desires and words in scripture. Instead of giving up fairly inconsequential things for Lent, grant me the head and the heart of the prophets of justice who knew that true fasting is the length of time and the considerable effort required to 'remove the yoke of affliction' from the necks of people, and who also knew that 'worship without justice has no value.' May I not be guilty of the 'false accusation and malicious speech' which continue to damage society and church. Help me to do the best I can, alone and with others, to 'satisfy the needs of the afflicted'. I make my prayer through Christ our Lord. Amen.

1st Sunday of Lent

Blessed Disruption

Scripture passage

And the Spirit immediately drove [Jesus] out into the wilderness. He was in the wilderness for forty days, tempted by Satan; and he was with wild beasts; and the angels waited on him. Now after John was arrested, Jesus came to Galilee, proclaiming the good news of God, and saying, 'The time is fulfilled, and the kingdom of God has come near; repent, and believe in the good news.'
(Mk 1:12-15)

Reflection

Everything Jesus did in his ministry was done under the guidance of the Holy Spirit. And so the Spirit directs Jesus into the wilderness 'for forty days' to be tempted, or tested, by Satan. We are undergoing our forty days of Lent. Our Lenten wilderness may be mild by comparison, but it is our way of patterning our lives on Jesus' life and showing solidarity with him. We may rest assured that the Lord appreciates our good will and our effort.

The Satan who tests Jesus tests us too. And all the time. Satan appears in scripture in several guises and, hence, is understood in scripture in different ways. In the Book of Job, for example, he is 'a son of God' and a reporter of human weakness as if he were on God's payroll! In the gospels, however, he is God's greatest enemy. In Hebrew, Satan means 'the adversary'. Sometimes in scripture Satan is a person or a personal entity; other times Satan stands for darkness and collective evil. The scholar William Barclay describes Satan as 'the essence of everything that is against God'. (*Daily Study Bible: Mark*) Since we try to align our lives with God's will, we are necessarily caught up in the struggle against Satan and with everything that is against God. Lent reminds us of our struggle, and the fasting and discipline of Lent are intended to hone our spiritual skills for the struggle.

The testing of Jesus in the wilderness was the prelude to his announcement of the 'good news of God.' The good news is the news of the arrival of the kingdom of God in the person and through the teachings of Jesus. The kingdom of God penetrates and disrupts people's lives. Penetration means the breaking into people's hearts of God's rule and grace, and disruption is the change which this now causes in thinking and manner of living. To accept the kingdom requires our personal decision in its favour, an about-face in our processes of thinking and ways of living, a new direction, and a commitment to the word of God in all we say and do. It begins with the call to repent, the call to leave the old behind and to embrace the new. Lent is a time to ask ourselves if we have left all of the old behind, and how deeply we have embraced the kingdom of the new.

Prayer
Father in heaven: May your kingdom come! May it come especially in my heart ever more and more and your word direct my whole being more and more. May your will be done in all that I say and do. May I see Satan as 'the essence of everything that is against you.' May I see every temptation as a test of my allegiance to you. May I endure all my tests. May I overcome all my temptations. I ask this in the name of your beloved Son and through the power of your Holy Spirit. Amen.

Activity for the first week of Lent
Visit a relative who is overdue a visit. Or, look in on a neighbour who is elderly and alone. Ask how you might help them and discreetly note the condition of such items as locks, lights, leaks, heat and fire alarms.

Monday of the first week of Lent

The Call to be Holy

Scripture passage

> The Lord spoke to Moses, saying: Speak to all the congreg-
> ation of the people of Israel, and say to them: You shall be
> holy, for I the Lord your God am holy.
> (Lev 19:1-2)

Reflection

The highest calling of a chosen people is to be holy as the Lord
their God is holy. It is so easy for us in the church community to
forget this amid the rumble of theological argument, liturgical
change, and the rush of documents and devotions, messengers
and messages of all kinds. But we must listen to this word of
God because it is emphatic: 'You shall make and keep yourselves holy, for I, the Lord your God, am holy.' (Lev 11:44)

When God chose the Hebrew people of old, he did so in
order to fashion for himself a people different from all the other
peoples of the earth, and particularly like himself. The distin-
guishing mark of this people would be their holiness. Of you
and me, the new people of God, Paul writes, 'God has saved us
and has called us to a holy life.' (2 Tim 1:9) Peter says, 'As he
who called you is holy, be holy yourselves in all your conduct;
for it is written, "You shall be holy, for I am holy".' (1 Pet 1:15)
And he adds, 'You are a chosen race, a royal priesthood, a holy
nation, a people God claims for his own.' (2 Pet 2:9)

The way of holiness is the way we must go. And the way of
holiness is the way of love. Our scripture passage is taken from
that section of the Book of Leviticus called 'the holiness code'. It
is a very long section. The holiness code spells out all the obligations in love required of a people who are in a covenant, or
sacred pact, with their God. In similar, but shorter, fashion, the
Ten Commandments spell out our obligations in love to God
and to those around us. Jesus identified the substance and heart
of these Ten Commandments when he said, 'You shall love the

Lord your God with all your heart ... You shall love your neighbour as yourself.' (Mt 22:37, 39)

Love, then, is the essence of what we are about, and of holiness. St. Thérèse of Lisieux, the Little Flower behind her convent walls, knew that she did not have the opportunity of doing the great deeds of love that are accessible to missionaries and martyrs in distant lands. And she sensed that her life would be a short one. So she chose what she called 'the little way' of holiness. It is the way of love. She said to her beloved Jesus: 'Love proves itself by deeds, and how shall I prove mine? [This] little child will scatter flowers whose fragrant perfume will surround the royal throne ... I can prove my love only by scattering flowers, that is to say, by never letting slip a single little sacrifice, a single glance, a single word; by making profit of the very smallest actions, by doing them all for love.' (*Autobiography: The Story of a Soul*) Thérèse's little way of love to holiness is within the capacity of any and all of us.

Prayer
Dear St Thérèse of Lisieux: Help me to see holiness as the normal way of life for a child of God. Help me understand that holiness reflects God's wholeness or completeness. Becoming the whole person which God desires me to become is possible through my transformation in Christ, following his way and his words in the gospels, and utilising his graces. It is not a huge mountain to be climbed but a dedicated way of love to be lived. Encourage me in your 'little way'. Let my way be little in being full of small things and minor moments, only let each of these be met by me with an intensity of love patterned on your own. Kindly confirm me in your belief that 'He does not need our works, only our love.' Thank you. Amen.

Tuesday of the first week of Lent

Potent Words

Scripture passage

> For as the rain and the snow come down from heaven,
> and do not return there until they have watered the earth,
> making it bring forth and sprout,
> giving seed to the sower and bread to the eater,
> so shall my word be that goes out from my mouth;
> it shall not return to me empty,
> but it shall accomplish that which I purpose,
> and succeed in the thing for which I sent it.
> (Isa 55:10-11)

Reflection

God's word is always effective. It does not return to God empty. It accomplishes the purpose for which he sends it. This is the thesis of our scripture passage. It is proven now as the exiles in Babylon prepare to return to Jerusalem. During their long captivity, 'by the waters of Babylon' (Ps 137:1), God sent them promises of return and of in-gathering again in their holy city of Jerusalem. God's promises are fulfilled now; God's word is proven effective.

Later in salvation history, God sent his word in the form of Jesus to be the word of reconciliation not only for his people Israel but 'for all the nations'. (Rom 1:5) 'And the Word became flesh and lived among us ... full of grace and truth.' (Jn 1:14) Jesus spoke effective words of reconciliation to all who would listen to him with a receptive ear and a responsive heart. He was a sower, he said, and the seed he sowed was the word of God. (cf Mt 13: 1-9, 18-23)

Then Jesus passed on responsibility for the word of reconciliation to us. 'God has given us the ministry of reconciliation,' writes Paul, 'entrusting the message of reconciliation to us. So we are ambassadors for Christ, since God is making his appeal through us.' (2 Cor 5:18-20) This word and ministry of reconciliation, which has been passed on to us, is a great responsibility indeed, but the grace of God goes with it. How shall we spread the word? How shall it be effective on our lips? The more we conform ourselves to the word of God, the more we become a living word of truth and grace ourselves, the more effective will be its going forth from us to others and not returning to him empty.

Prayer

Dear Jesus: May the word I speak in your name be an effective word. May my speech and actions be as the snow and the rain which fell on the parched fields of Israel and made them fruitful. May my words and deeds address the needs of all who cross my path. May they be words and deeds of enlightenment or of encouragement, of comfort or of peace, of justice or of forgiveness, as needs be. May I always address people where they are in their struggles and in their journey of faith. May I always speed them on their way with the word or the action that supports and blesses them. Amen.

Wednesday of the first week of Lent

Attend to the Lord!

Scripture passage

When the crowds were increasing, [Jesus] began to say, 'This generation is an evil generation; it asks for a sign, but no sign will be given to it except the sign of Jonah. For just as Jonah became a sign to the people of Nineveh, so the Son of Man will be to this generation. The queen of the South will rise at the judgement with the people of this generation and condemn them, because she came from the ends of the earth to listen to the wisdom of Solomon, and see, something greater than Solomon is here! The people of Nineveh will rise up at the judgement with this generation and condemn it, because they repented at the proclamation of Jonah, and see, something greater than Jonah is here!'

(Lk 11:29-32)

Reflection

Jonah lived about the fifth century before Christ. This was the time after the exile in Babylon when the restored community, and its prophets, should be expressing wide-hearted gratitude to God for their deliverance. But they have grown inward. Even the prophet Jonah closes his heart to God's call that he go to the great and sinful city of Nineveh 'and cry out against it.' (Jon 1:2) It is possible that Jonah acted from excessive humility rather than hardness of heart. At any rate, he refuses God by closing his heart to the call. He flees instead by ship and – to shorten the story – ends up 'in the belly of a large fish.' (Jon 1:17) But he learns his lesson: Don't run from God! Don't avoid your spiritual task! Jonah finally goes and calls Nineveh to repentance. He is shocked to find that Nineveh listens to him and repents!

In our scripture passage, Jesus is engaged by people seeking a great sign which will prove to them – on their terms – that he is the Messiah. He refuses. And well he might, for his teaching already bears the marks of a great prophet, and his mission is already authenticated by many signs and wonders. Jesus makes reference to the prophet Jonah. For all of Jonah's weakness (or humility) and disobedience, the people of Nineveh listened to him, accepted him as a prophet from God and acted on his word. Yet Jesus' hearers will not accept Jesus even though his signs and miracles already show that in him 'something greater than Jonah is here.' The far-distant Queen of Sheba came all the way to Jerusalem to listen to the wisdom of King Solomon, acting on the mere rumour of it, yet a 'greater than Solomon' stands before the people in the person of Jesus. It is for such reasons that Jesus tells his stubborn hearers, who keep wanting an extra-special sign, that on the Day of Judgement Sheba's pagan queen and Nineveh's converted sinners will condemn them for not accepting the one who stands before them; one who is far greater and more critical to their spiritual journey and to their eternal destiny than any and every Solomon and Jonah.

Prayer

Dear Jesus: May I never demand extra-special signs from you on my faith journey! May I never stop following you and listening to your words in the gospel and in our quiet spiritual communion together. My world (as you well know) is full of words and voices of all kinds, promoting all manner of product, by every method of presentation and psychology of persuasion. Let yours be the words I continue to listen to, and hear the best. Let yours be the saving voice calling me to true liberty, to real life, and to my eternal destiny. Amen.

Thursday of the first week of Lent

The Golden Rule

Scripture passage

> [Jesus said], 'In everything, do to others as you would have them do to you; this is the law and the prophets.'
> (Mt 7:12)

Reflection

This teaching of our Lord is known to generations of Christians as 'the Golden Rule.' Jesus teaches that this rule, or standard of behaviour, sums up the Law of God and the teachings of the prophets as well. We should treat people in the manner we wish to be treated ourselves. And, of course, since we all wish to be treated only in the best possible manner, we should treat others precisely the same way.

Is this very expansive ethic a bridge too far? For the world of greed and grasping, of course it is! For the world of guns and ruthlessness, of course it is! For the world of malice and revenge, of course it is! For the world of the narrow mind and the fearful heart, of course it is! But such worlds are not properly human worlds. The Golden Rule is no more than normal behaviour in the world of the kingdom of God.

The Golden Rule is found in the teachings of many philosophers, such as Confucius and Philo, and in various books of wisdom, though usually in negative forms, such as in the book of Tobit where it reads, 'Do not do to anyone what you yourself dislike.' (Tob 4:15)

Jesus' version of the Rule is not only positively stated but infers a number of things which are not evident at first glance. One inference is that we treat others – precisely – as we would like to be treated ourselves. A second inference is that we treat them in this manner irrespective of how they treat us now or may treat us in the future. And a third is that we should act all the time, irrespective of the circumstances, from the basis of the Golden Rule as though it were second nature to us. Jesus does not call us to faulty versions of the Golden Rule such as, 'Scratch my back and I'll scratch yours' (as in the world of the primates!), or 'You get what you give' (as in the underworld of paid protection!), or 'I'll treat you right when you learn to behave.' These sentiments are no more than modern adaptations of the old eye-for-an-eye and tooth-for-a-tooth mantra.

When it comes to understanding the Golden Rule in our lives, we need to see it in the light of Jesus' theology of turning the other cheek, of going the extra mile, and of giving one's cloak in addition to one's tunic. (cf Mt 5:38-42) Or, as William Barclay puts it, 'The Christian ethic is based on the extra thing.' (*Daily Study Bible: Luke*)

Prayer

Father: Your Son's teaching called the Golden Rule is sometimes described as 'over the top' or excessively idealistic. It seems so removed from what is called real life. Can it have a place in our highly competitive and aggressive society? Kindly remind me that your Son spoke his Rule, his ethic of the extra thing, in a similarly competitive and aggressive environment and from the basis of a personal life under constant siege from the whispers, the stonewalling, the insults and the rejection of those he would die to save. This is the realism that grounds his Golden Rule. So your beloved Son has every right to set it as the standard of behaviour for his true followers. Allow me to appreciate this. And give me the heart to try my best to live it. I make my prayer through Christ our Lord. Amen.

Friday of the first week of Lent

The Spirit of Religion

Scripture passage

[Jesus said], 'Unless your righteousness exceeds that of the scribes and Pharisees, you will never enter the kingdom of heaven.'
(Mt 5:20)

Reflection

Our scripture passage is a small segment of our Lord's Sermon on the Mount. His teaching is directed at his followers and would-be followers. In the Sermon, he is about his declared task of not abolishing the Law of God but of bringing it to completion. (cf Mt 5:17) This involves teaching the Law properly and emphasising its spirit in contrast to the rules-and-regulations approach of the scribes and the Pharisees. Two different levels of righteousness, or of ethical behaviour, are achieved by the two contrasting interpretations of the Law, and Jesus is in no doubt as to which is the superior one. He says, 'Unless your righteousness [i.e. your goodness before God and your justice in respect of others] exceeds that of the scribes and Pharisees, you will never enter the kingdom of heaven.' (The kingdom of heaven is the phrasing Matthew uses occasionally for the kingdom of God.)

We see the difference between Jesus' emphasis on the spirit of the Law and the rigorous, regulating mentality of the scribes and Pharisees in many gospel incidents, and in most of the recorded conflicts between them and Jesus. For example, Jesus healed needy people on the sabbath, and the scribes and Pharisees called him a Law-breaker. Yet is not the Law properly summed-up in love of God and love of neighbour? And who is my neighbour? My neighbour is any fellow human being in need, and when he or she is in need, even if that happens to be on the sabbath, 'the Lord's day' and 'the day of rest'. Besides, who were these falsely righteous scribes and Pharisees? The scholar William Barclay calls the scribes 'a race of men who made it the business of their lives to reduce the great principles of the Law to literally thousands upon thousands of rules and regulations.' As to the Pharisees, they were men who then 'separated themselves from all the ordinary activities of life to keep all these rules and regulations.' (*Daily Study Bible: Matthew*)

Living the Law of God according to its spirit can never involve the rigorous mentality, or be a matter of multiplying rules and regulations. These only damage the integrity of the Law; they undermine its spirit; and they overburden God's people. Living the Law of God according to its spirit means living our lives in the ways and means of justice, love and caring as Jesus, the fulfiller of the Law and its exemplar, did so beautifully before us.

Prayer

Lord Jesus: May we not undermine your teaching by overburdening it with our rules and regulations. We realise that some rules and regulations are necessary in every life and in every society, including the church. But save us from the over-ruled and rigid life which only deadens the spirit. May we take note of Chesterton's remark that a religion which interferes more than it ought is a dying one, and may we attend well to your words: 'God is spirit, and those who worship him must worship in spirit and in truth.' (Jn 4:24) Amen.

Saturday of the first week of Lent

Stretching Our Love

Scripture passage

[Jesus said], 'You have heard that it was said, "You shall love your neighbour and hate your enemy." But I say to you, Love your enemies and pray for those who persecute you, so that you may be children of your Father in heaven; for he makes his sun rise on the evil and on the good, and sends rain on the righteous and on the unrighteous. For if you love those who love you, what reward do you have? Do not even the tax-collectors do the same? And if you greet only your brothers and sisters, what more are you doing than others? Do not even the Gentiles do the same? Be perfect, therefore, as your heavenly Father is perfect.'

(Mt 5:43-48)

Reflection

Jesus says, 'You have heard that it was said, "You shall love your neighbour and hate your enemy".' We do not know what official or popular 'scripture' our Lord is referring to when he says, 'You have heard that it was said.' He may be referring to an old interpretation of the commandment of love of neighbour by which one's immediate neighbours were to be loved, but strangers held at arm's length, and enemies simply hated! I suppose all of this is understandable from the point of view of weak human nature. But such was never God's intention for the law of love. Jesus says, 'I say to you, love your enemies and pray for those who persecute you.'

Jesus bases his expansive understanding of the commandment, and the necessity of our expansive love for others, not on the basis of kin, nationality, or even true religion but on the fact that we are all 'children of your Father' and should act as all-inclusively as he does. He is the Father of all, not of some, 'for he makes his sun rise on the evil and on the good, and sends rain on the righteous and on the unrighteous.' (Mt 5:45) Jesus wants us to love even our enemies and those who harm us, says John P. Meier, 'simply because that is the way the Father acts.' (*New Testament Message: Matthew*)

Now instinct and common sense tell us that we cannot love enemies in the same way that we love spouse, children, relatives, close friends and immediate neighbours. And we know that even the best fathers and mothers love their children deeply but yet may yet reproach them and call them to account. So what is Jesus asking of us in asking us to love our enemies? Perhaps goodwill to begin with. Perhaps a greater tolerance. And perhaps, if we are given the chance, some effort at correcting and rehabilitating our enemies – instead of wanting to wipe them out! The biblical scholars generally are sure of one thing: loving our enemies means, at the very least, banishing our hatred and our yearning for revenge.

Prayer

Dear Father: Please grant me an expansive love. Let my heart have room for more than those I call 'my own' and 'our own'. May I see all people as your children, no matter how different they are, or how strange they seem, or how poorly I think they behave. You are their Father as well as my Father: you are our Father. Deaden in me the natural instinct to name my enemies, to hate them, and to desire revenge. Help me to open my heart wide after the manner of your beloved Son, and grant me my measure of the great social grace of an enduring tolerance. I ask this in the name of Jesus and as a special direction of the Holy Spirit in my life. Amen.

Second Sunday of Lent

Are You Saved?

Scripture passage

'The word is near to you, on your lips and in your heart' (that is, the word of faith that we proclaim); because if you confess with your lips that Jesus is Lord and believe in your heart that God raised him from the dead, you will be saved. For one believes with the heart and so is justified, and one confesses with the mouth and so is saved. The scripture says, 'No one who believes in him shall be put to shame.' For there is no distinction between Jew and Greek; the same Lord is Lord of all and is generous to all who call on him. For, 'Everyone who calls on the name of the Lord shall be saved.' (Rom 10:8-13)

Reflection

Many of us, especially if we have lived abroad, are familiar with the knock on the door and the strange voice asking, 'Brother/ Sister, are you saved?' When we hear it the first time we are taken by surprise. Perhaps we even feel a bit insulted. We say, 'What do you mean 'saved'? I'm a committed Catholic!' as though that should be the end of that. But the confident voice continues, 'A Catholic? Then you really must listen to me, Brother/Sister.' The notion is still fairly common that Catholics are people of the half-light, who tend to believe in anything and everything, and especially in the pope and Mary.

The apostle Paul says in our scripture passage, 'If you confess with your lips that Jesus is Lord and believe in your heart that God raised him from the dead, you will be saved.' There is no talk here of pope or Mary or a myriad of other 'Catholic things'. The voice at the door has a point.

Who is St Paul addressing, and what is his point? He is addressing the Christian community in Rome which he is about to visit. They are a mix of Jewish and Gentile converts. Paul wishes to confirm their faith in 'the new way' of Jesus and the gospel.

He does this by stressing the gospel over the prescriptions of the old Law as the way to be saved. He underlines the importance of faith in Jesus as Saviour and in Jesus as the now resurrected Lord in glory. Saviour and Lord! This is Paul's capsule theology of salvation – if I may call it that – or essence of Christian faith. How should I respond to it?

I respond on two levels. First, as a member of the faith community, I involve myself in the wonderful liturgical life of the church. The liturgy, day by day, season by season, and year by year remembers, re-tells and re-lives the life, death and resurrection of Jesus as our communal Saviour and Lord. In the liturgy, we confess and affirm our faith in Jesus as our Saviour and our Lord over and over again. And second, I personally accept Jesus as my sole Saviour and Lord, not only believing this in my heart of hearts but trying to live it out in my words and encounters and actions as best I can day by day, season by season, and year by year. I desire this paired response to be my response both to St Paul's capsule theology of salvation and to the insistent, but well-meaning, voice at the door.

Prayer
Jesus: I accept you as my Saviour and Lord. I thank you for allowing me to call you my Saviour and my Lord. And I thank you for the family members, the parish community, and the Christian friends of different traditions with whom I gather for teaching, study and prayer, who joyfully name you their Saviour and their Lord. Confirm all of us in our faith and in our love for you. And let nothing ever separate us from you. Amen.

Activity for the second week of Lent
I re-dedicate myself to the liturgy and to being an active participant in the communal worship of our God. And this week I will offer to clean an elderly person's home or to give a caring neighbour a few hours' respite, knowing this may leave me open to future calls.

Monday of the second week of Lent

Sin as Treachery

Scripture passage

'Ah, Lord, great and awesome God, keeping covenant and steadfast love with those who love you and keep your commandments, we have sinned and done wrong, acted wickedly and rebelled, turning aside from your commandments and ordinances. We have not listened to your servants the prophets, who spoke in your name to our kings, our princes, and our ancestors, and to all the people of the land. Righteousness is on your side, O Lord, but open shame, as at this day, falls on us ... because of the treachery that [we] have committed against you.'
(Dan 9:4-7)

Reflection

Daniel, from whose book our scripture passage is taken, was a Jewish captive among the exiles in Babylon and a hero of his people. He is perhaps best known to most of us as the young man who interprets the dreams of the pagan King Nebuchadnezzar and, later, the famous 'writing on the wall' that terrifies King Belshazzar (Nebuchadnezzar's son) and signals the downfall of his house.

In our scripture passage, Daniel 'interprets' the captivity of God's people in Babylon. Why are they there and not at home with God in Jerusalem where they belong? There is only one answer: they are where they are because they have sinned. Daniel's understanding of sin may catch our attention. Sin is not just a matter of breaking God's law or offending him and others. Sin – for a covenanted people – is rebellion. Sin – for a people married to the Lord – is infidelity. Either way, sin is 'treachery'. (v. 7)

Daniel says that this treachery has come about in part because the people have not listened to God's servants the prophets. Many generations later, Jesus tells the story of the insensitive rich man and the poor man Lazarus. When Lazarus dies he is carried by angels 'to be with Abraham'. When the insensitive rich man dies he finds himself 'in Hades'. The rich man wants Abraham to send Lazarus, or someone else, from the dead in order to convince his still-living brothers to repent lest they end up in Hades too. But Abraham answers, 'They have Moses and the prophets; they should listen to them.' (cf Lk 16: 19-31)

We, also, have the words of Moses and the prophets in the scriptures to listen to, to light our path and direct our lives. And we have much more. We have Jesus the Word of God made man. The author of the Letter to the Hebrews writes: 'Long ago God spoke to our ancestors in many and various ways by the prophets, but in these last days he has spoken to us by a Son.' (Heb 1:1-2) We have the full directing word of God in Jesus, and abounding grace through Christ, to safeguard us from treachery.

Prayer
Heavenly Father: We moderns have trouble in accepting our sinfulness and in identifying our sins. Sin means little to a lot of people: excuse and cover-up mean a lot more. Grant us Christians the sense of sin as infidelity to your enduring love. Grant us the sense of sin as large or small treacheries to our baptismal promises and to our sublime calling in Christ. Do not let us be tempted by the popular notion that the only sin is being caught. Impress on us the truth that no sin, whether social or personal, is victimless. I make my prayer through Christ our Lord. Amen.

Tuesday of the second week of Lent

True Repentance

Scripture passage
> Come now, let us argue it out,
> says the Lord:
> though your sins are like scarlet,
> they shall be like snow;
> though they are red like crimson,
> they shall become as wool.
> If you are willing and obedient,
> you shall eat the good of the land;
> but if you refuse and rebel,
> you shall be devoured by the sword;
> for the mouth of the Lord has spoken.
> (Isa 1:18-20)

Reflection
In this passage we come upon one of the best known and best loved lines of scripture. God says, 'Come now, let us set things right: Though your sins be like scarlet, they shall become white as snow; though they be crimson red, they may become white as wool.' (NAB version) In context, this lovely line is spoken as contrast and then complement to the lines, 'your hands are full of blood. Wash yourselves clean!' (Isa 1:15-16)

We may imagine God coming down to our level, so to speak, putting his encouraging hand on our shoulder and saying, 'Now in the matter of your sins, and no matter how bad they are, I'm here to assure you that if you are genuinely contrite and start living your life by the commandments which I devised for your happiness, you can be a very changed person.' We can imagine God then pointing to two background images – the snowy slopes of the mountains of Lebanon to the north and the pure white wool on the backs of the spring lambs in the pastures – and saying encouragingly, 'Even if your soul be now bloodied red from your sins, it can become as white as the lamb's wool and as pure as the mountain snow.' And all because there is no end to God's mercy!

Isaiah's purpose, in speaking these lines on behalf of God, is to engender true repentance in God's people then and in ourselves now. To refuse such an inviting repentance is a sign of rebellion, and rebellion against God's will is the core of any and all biblical sin. Rebellion was the pivotal aspect of the sin of the angels and of Adam. The rebellious angels were driven from heaven by Michael, 'wielding his sword', and fallen man was driven from the garden of Eden, the angels thereafter guarding its boundaries and 'a flaming sword' blocking the way back. (cf Gen 3:22-24) Hence, Isaiah is able to say to his hearers back then, and says to us now, ' If you refuse to repent and rebel, you shall be devoured by the sword.' Our refusal to repent is the sword that devours us. It is a sword of our own making.

Prayer
Father: Forgive me my sins as I forgive those who sin against me! There is no honest life that is not aware of its sin, and there is no life lived with faith that refuses to acknowledge its yearly and even daily sin. When I sin, let me return to you with all my heart. Remind me of your saving and loving words: 'Come now, let us set things right. Though your sins be like scarlet, they shall become white as snow; though they be crimson red, they may become white as wool.' I thank you, Father, for your tender mercy, through Christ our Lord. Amen.

Wednesday of the second week of Lent

Patterns of Leadership

Scripture passage

Then the mother of the sons of Zebedee came to [Jesus] with her sons, and kneeling before him, she asked a favour of him. And he said to her, 'What do you want?' She said to him, 'Declare that these two sons of mine will sit, one at your right hand and one at your left, in your kingdom.' ... When the ten heard it, they were angry with the two brothers. But Jesus called them to him and said, 'You know that the rulers of the Gentiles lord it over them, and their great ones are tyrants over them. It will not be so among you; but whoever wishes to be great among you must be your servant, and whoever wishes to be first among you must be your slave; just as the Son of Man came not to be served but to serve, and to give his life a ransom for many.'
(Mt 20: 20, 21, 24-28)

Reflection

We may be shocked to hear this mother ask for high positions for her two sons in the government of God's kingdom. If we are shocked, perhaps it's because we know more about the spiritual nature of the kingdom of God than did she – and her sons – at the time of her request. She presumed that the kingdom would be more or less a kingdom of this world with similar cabinet posts. It is natural that she would want her two boys to be prominent in the government. What mother wouldn't! In Mark's gospel, the two sons are identified as the apostles James and John (cf Mk 10:35-45), and they are cousins of Jesus. This makes the mother's request even more understandable: she may have assumed that ties of kinship gave her a special right of request.

At any rate, Jesus uses the incident to speak about the Christian way and its new form of leadership. Old patterns of behaviour and old styles of leadership must give way a new one, and the new one is the opposite of the old. Whoever wants to be great in the kingdom of God must become the servant of others. Whoever wants to rank first must become the slave of all. In sum, lordly power means nothing in the kingdom, but humble service everything. Jesus offers himself as our model. He is the Messiah of God. He is the Word of God incarnate. John – one of Zebedee's sons! – later writes: 'All things came into being through him, and without him not one thing came into being.' (Jn 1:3) He has, then, the right to our obedience and to our obeisance, yet he came among us 'not to be served but to serve, even to give his life a ransom for many.' (Mk 10:45)

We are familiar with this teaching of Jesus with regard to leadership in the kingdom of God, i.e. with regard to Christian leadership. The church community knows the teaching well. We preach it and write documents about it. But do we put it into practice? We find it hard to leave the old way, to let go of the old imperial pattern, old psychologies of lordship, and old styles of leadership however much we think the Second Vatican Council wished to foreclose on them. A time of crisis and perplexity, such as the one we've experienced recently with the child abuse saga, reveals whether the old patterns and styles of church leadership have really died or just hidden themselves away in a corner to reappear when confrontation comes calling.

Prayer
Father: Forgive me the times I lorded it over your children in the church community because of my position of authority or influence. Forgive me the times I dismissed the Spirit's counsel in favour of my own. Forgive the poorly prepared lecture, the rushed homily, the uncertain advice. And forgive the higher authorities of the church of recent years and of past ages. May ours not be the legacy of the mixed message and the damaged blessing. Renew and direct all in church life, in civic life, and in home life who are called to the service of leading and caring for others. Kindly heed my prayer through Christ our Lord. Amen.

Thursday of the second week of Lent

True Wisdom

Scripture passage

Thus says the Lord:

Cursed are those who trust in mere mortals

and make mere flesh their strength,

whose hearts turn away from the Lord.

They shall be like a shrub in the desert,

and shall not see when relief comes.

They shall live in the parched places of the wilderness,

in an uninhabited salt land.

Blessed are those who trust in the Lord,

whose trust is the Lord.

They shall be like a tree planted by water,

sending out its roots by the stream.

It shall not fear when heat comes,

and its leaves shall stay green;

in the year of drought it is not anxious,

and it does not cease to bear fruit.

(Jer 17:5-8)

Reflection

Jeremiah's words are directed at Jerusalem and Judah, but they may be applied to all of us who are pledged to the Lord yet may be tempted to trust others rather than him in our need and in crisis. When Jerusalem and Judah should have relied on their Lord, they relied on pagan alliances instead. When they should have followed the wisdom of the Lord's ways, they followed human calculation instead. They have lost. Banishment to Babylon is their lot. The prophet sees their sin as near indelible, written 'on the tablets of their hearts,' i.e. on hearts of stone. (See Jer 17:1)

Jeremiah's call to repentance takes the form of teaching the people the dissimilarity of true wisdom and false wisdom. True wisdom is following the Lord and his ways: false wisdom is deserting God and his ways and preferring human intrigue. Jeremiah uses familiar images in his teaching. Those who abandon God and rely on 'mere mortals' are like a shrub living 'in the wilderness.' The shrub withers for lack of moisture. On the other hand, those who trust in the Lord are 'like a tree planted by water, sending out its roots to the stream.' The watered tree never ceases 'to bear fruit.' The inference is that God is the source of the life-giving water, and the water represents true wisdom. For Jeremiah, true wisdom is the knowledge of the ways of the Lord and the following of those ways. For you and me, true wisdom also is the knowledge of the ways of the Lord, but now in their plenitude of understanding and grace through Christ.

Prayer

Lord God: Jeremiah's words may not be used to put down human wisdom, but human folly. Human wisdom benefits us as philosophy, art, science, medicine and technology. Wisdom is a house of many wonderful rooms. And all wisdom comes from you. Jeremiah speaks to the people you called your own. He is merely stressing that a covenanted people should rely on you and on the covenant, not on pagan alliances and passing military muscle. So do not allow believers to put down science and technology (as they sometimes tend to do) as though these were of no consequence to our well-being, or opposed to your will and the attainment of all of your purposes. Rather, fix us in the truth that your beloved Son Jesus is a special Word, a unique Wisdom, our saving word and wisdom in this life and for our eternal happiness. Amen.

Friday of the second week of Lent

New Tenants

Scripture passage

[Jesus said], 'Listen to another parable. There was a landowner who planted a vineyard, put a fence around it, dug a wine press in it, and built a watch-tower. Then he leased it to tenants and went to another country. When the harvest time had come, he sent his slaves to the tenants to collect his produce. But the tenants seized his slaves and beat one, killed another, and stoned another. Again he sent other slaves, more than the first; and they treated them in the same way. Finally he sent his son to them, saying, "They will respect my son." But when the tenants saw the son, they said to themselves, "This is the heir; come, let us kill him and get his inheritance." So they seized him, threw him out of the vineyard, and killed him. Now when the owner of the vineyard comes, what will he do to those tenants? They said to him, "He will put those wretches to a miserable death, and lease the vineyard to other tenants who will give him the produce at the harvest time".'
(Mt 21:33-41)

Reflection

Jesus spoke this parable for anyone with ears to hear, but he meant it especially for the Pharisees and the religious leaders of Israel. One scripture scholar calls it a parable of judgement on Israel; another a parable of doom for that nation. The landowner who planted the vineyard is God and the vineyard is Israel. 'For the vineyard of the Lord of hosts,' says the prophet Isaiah, 'is the house of Israel.' (Isa 5:7) Jesus gives the details of the vineyard more or less as they are given by Isaiah. (cf Isa 5:2) For example, the 'fence' is a hedge to keep out roving animals and the 'watch-tower' serves to guard against thieves. William Barclay suggests that the workers also slept in it. The vineyard is 'leased to tenants.' These are the Pharisees and the other religious leaders of

Israel. The 'slaves' ('servants' in some translations) sent to 'collect the produce' at harvest time are the prophets God sent to assess the progress of God's people in holiness and justice, and to re-align them as needed. The prophets are consistently rejected, stoned or killed. Finally, God sends his Son. 'They will respect my son,' he says. But Jesus is aware that they will not. Instead, they will kill him. Consequently, judgement and doom befall 'those wretches'. Jerusalem is destroyed and the religious leadership of Israel loses favour with God. The Lord's vineyard is now entrusted to 'other tenants.' We Christians read 'other tenants' to mean ourselves as the church, i.e. all of us collectively but in differing ways, with our variety of talents, and various levels and degrees of leadership and responsibility. The church will now produce 'the harvest of justice, the good works God wills.' (John P. Meier, *New Testament Message: Matthew*)

We, as the church community, are entrusted with the kingdom of God and its work on earth. We are called to be the committed and productive tenants who yield the harvest of holiness and justice, 'the good works that God desires.'

Prayer

Dearest Jesus: We tend to take things for granted. The leaders, priests and shepherds of Israel took things for granted. They were the appointed ones. They were the anointed ones. They proved to be the disappointing ones. They did not cultivate the vineyard of your Father so as to make it productive. They did not give the flock of God sufficient care. They worshipped the Father with their lips, but not sufficiently with their hearts. Forgive me for seeing much of myself and my life in this history. And forgive our church leadership for aspects of the same. Make us pay more attention to your directing words in the gospels than to our own assessments as to how the vineyard should be tended and the flock shepherded. May all of us be productive tenants to please our loving Father. Amen.

Saturday of the second week of Lent

Shepherding

Scripture passage
> Shepherd your people with your staff,
> the flock that belongs to you,
> which lives alone in a forest
> in the midst of a garden land;
> let them feed in Bashan and Gilead
> as in the days of old.
> As in the days when you came out of
> the land of Egypt,
> show us marvellous things.
> (Mic 7:14-15)

Reflection

The book of the prophet Micah is short but powerful. He was a contemporary of Isaiah. He was trenchant in his condemnation of civil and religious corruption in Israel. As is usual in the scriptures, it is the well-off and the leaders, not the little people, who are the main object of the prophet's tongue-lashing. He takes the rich to task for exploiting the poor. He attacks defrauding merchants, dishonest judges, corrupt priests and wayward prophets. Social evils and unacknowledged guilt are widespread in the nation and Micah predicts the collapse of the leadership. But God will have compassion on the little people, and show them clemency, and Israel will be restored.

Sentences with which we are very familiar are found in Micah. In the liturgy of Good Friday, for instance, we visualise the battered and sorrowful Christ saying to our sinful selves what God through Micah says to Israel: 'O my people, what have I done to you? In what have I offended you? Answer me!' (Mic 6:3) And – for us in Advent – the foretelling of the birth of our Saviour with the heartening line: 'But you, O Bethlehem of Ephrathah, who are one of the little clans of Judah, from you shall come forth for me one who is to rule in Israel, whose origin is from of old, from ancient days.' (Mic 5:2) With this text, Micah foresees the return of good shepherds and good shepherding to Israel, and we see the coming of the Good Shepherd.

When one reads a little history, or even the limited but indicative history which is extractable from a prophetical book such as Micah, one realises the huge responsibility that rests on the shoulders of leadership of all kinds, whether this leadership and responsibility be on the world stage or not, whether it be in church or state, in business or health care, in office or classroom, in a rural setting or in the most modest of homes. We each have a flock, in one sense or another, to serve. We are each responsible for a measure of shepherding in one form or another. So we listen carefully to the challenge of Micah, and look to see the place and the persons of our shepherding. They are always at our elbow. 'Shepherd your people with your staff, the flock that belongs to you!' Shepherd them whether they live 'alone in a forest' of urban fear or 'in the midst of a garden land' of rural peace.

Prayer

Dearest Jesus: You are the shepherd of shepherds, the Good Shepherd, the model shepherd of Israel. Every one of us cares for the flock in one way or another. We all have people entrusted to our care, for whom we are responsible, whether we be priest, teacher, physician, Garda, politician, parent or grandparent. Shepherding faith, our own and that of others, in this time of weakened faith is very challenging. And so is shepherding spousal love and family life in this time of love's questioning and added threats to life. Look most kindly on all who shepherd in any way during these rather brittle days. And thank you for your own model shepherding of us. Amen.

Third Sunday of Lent

Cleaning House

Scripture passage

The Passover of the Jews was near, and Jesus went up to Jerusalem. In the temple he found people selling cattle, sheep, and doves, and the money-changers seated at their tables. Making a whip of cords, he drove all of them out of the temple, both the sheep and the cattle. He also poured out the coins of the money-changers and overturned their tables. He told those selling the doves, 'Take these things out of here! Stop making my Father's house a market-place!' His disciples remembered that it was written, 'Zeal for your house will consume me.'

(Jn 2:13-17)

Reflection

The temple of Jerusalem was the great national sanctuary of God and his people. King David and King Solomon had built it. It was the centre of Jewish worship. It was destroyed by the Babylonians and rebuilt as the second temple by the exiles returning from their Babylonian captivity. In our Lord's time, it was undergoing further development by King Herod. For all of that, what did Jesus find when he went up to the temple to pray at Passover? He found his own people turning God's house into a market-place and a money exchange!

Our Lord 'drove them all out of the temple.' He said, 'Stop making my Father's house a market-place!' Our Lord was gripped with righteous anger. What so incensed him? Not the money-changing operation as such, for Jews from many countries came for the Passover with their foreign coins and this 'unclean' money had to be exchanged for 'clean' Jewish shekels. And not the animals as such, for these were required for temple offering and sacrifice.

William Barclay suggests that what angered Jesus was the take-over of liturgy by commerce. For example, there were two sets of animals; one set within the temple precincts and the other without. The animals inside were several times more costly than those outside. While this may have been a small matter to the wealthy, it was a huge one to the poor. But even in the case of the wealthy, why should religion fleece them financially? The poor were also fleeced financially when they bought outside the temple precincts because these animals were subject to a special inspection tax. And there was no guarantee the poor man's animal would pass the inspection. So he was forced to repeat the test and pay a second time. (Clearly, the rip-off culture is nothing new!) These crooked factors made the temple officials 'extremely wealthy men'. All of this constituted a chronic injustice, and it discriminated terribly against the poor. The particular money-changers, whose tables Jesus overturned, were likely associated with this unjust trafficking. Barclay concludes that Jesus was incensed at the gross mistreatment of the poor and with the fact that this whole temple scene had become 'worship without reverence.' (*Daily Study Bible: John*)

Jesus used the occasion to tell the Jews that there would be a new temple. But it would not be the third temple, fashioned as usual of cedar and stone. It would be one fashioned from his own suffering and resurrected body. True worship of the Father would pass through this new temple 'not made with human hands.' (Acts 17:24). Much later, the apostle Paul – in view of our incorporation into Christ – saw the church as the new temple of God, a temple of holiness and pleasing worship. (cf 1 Cor 3:16-17) And he reminds us that each of us is 'the temple of the Holy Spirit.' (1 Cor 6:19) So, we each have a temple to care for! May we cleanse the house of our heart with enthusiasm this Lent as Jesus cleansed his Father's house with ardent zeal.

Prayer
Heavenly Father: Help me to cleanse the house that is myself. Help me to cleanse my heart of every wayward tendency and my mind of vagrant thoughts so that I may focus on the saving gospel of your Son. May I not live in the past, sifting through old

opportunities missed and graces poorly utilised. Help me to live in the present, and with the hope of the future. May I be a temple of pleasing worship and love, to which you are most heartily invited, and in which you are honoured, and through which your children are served. I ask this grace through Christ our Lord. Amen.

Activity for the third week of Lent
Our homes are statements of ourselves. What kind of Christian does my home say I am? Does my home suggest that I am too comfortable a Christian and have set my heart mainly on the goods and values of this life? Is there a crucifix among the furnishings or some other sign that mine is a home not at all ashamed of the Christ who died to save me? Is there a Catholic paper or Christian magazine or journal in my home to balance the many media materials that inform my judgements, influence my voting patterns, and reflect my tastes? This week I will set right what may need to be set right in my Christian home.

Monday of the third week of Lent

Facing Rejection

Scripture passage

And [Jesus] said, 'Truly I tell you, no prophet is accepted in the prophet's home town. But the truth is, there were many widows in Israel in the time of Elijah, when the heaven was shut up for three years and six months, and there was a severe famine over all the land; yet Elijah was sent to none of them except to a widow at Zarephath in Sidon. There were also many lepers in Israel in the time of the prophet Elisha, and none of them was cleansed except Naaman the Syrian.' When they heard this, all in the synagogue were filled with rage. They got up, drove him out of the town, and led him to the brow of the hill on which their town was built, so that they might hurl him off the cliff. But he passed through the midst of them and went on his way.
(Lk 4:24-30)

Reflection

Our scripture passage deals with an incident which happened in Jesus' home town of Nazareth. He had gone into the synagogue, where he was well known, read a Messianic passage from the book of Isaiah, and implied that he was its fulfilment, i.e. that he was the long-awaited Prophet and Messiah foretold by Isaiah. The re-action to this good news was anything but enthusiastic! His hometown hearers passed it off with the remark, 'Isn't this the son of Joseph?' In other words, 'How can he make such a claim? Don't we know his family well! He's just one of us!'

This instant rejection of Jesus by his own townspeople obviously hurt him. So he said, 'No prophet is accepted in his home town.' And then he went on to illustrate his point in a manner which angered them intensely. God, he said, sent the prophets Elijah and Elisha not to their Jewish ancestors but to the hated Gentiles because the Gentiles accepted them and their ministry. In this manner, Jesus infers that he is equally a great prophet with Elijah and Elisha; that he is sent by God as they were; that he and his ministry are being rejected by his hearers as their ancestors rejected the ministry of Elijah and Elisha; and that he will turn, as Elijah and Elisha turned, to the Gentiles who will accept him. 'When they heard this, all in the synagogue were filled with rage ... and led him to the brow of the hill on which their town was built, so that they might hurl him off the cliff.'

There are many things we must choose, and many things we must forego, in our faithful following of Jesus and in our living in accord with his standards. There are many ways in which we are rejected by others because of our love and our loyalty to him. But let the chips fall where they may. Let us choose what must be chosen, and bear any rejection, with a peaceful heart and lovingly for our Lord. Our rejection will never match the rejection he faced in his hometown, nor will we be met with the intense rage that confronted him and that put his life in danger when 'they led him to the brow of the hill on which their town was built, so that they might hurl him off the cliff.'

Prayer

Dearest Jesus: You know how often I visualise all the gospel scenes in which you proved your enduring love for me. You know how much I thank you, from the core of my self, for allowing yourself to be insulted, rejected, subjected to silence and misunderstanding, threatened, denied, betrayed, condemned, sent on your suffering way, abandoned by all but the faithful few, humiliated on Calvary, crucified and hidden away in a tomb – for me! Therefore, whatever I must forego in my pilgrimage, and however much I am rejected or denied by others for your sake, I accept all of it with a full heart and as my poor effort to reciprocate your amazing love for me. Never stop loving me the way you love me! And kindly increase my love for you! Amen.

Tuesday of the third week of Lent

No Frontiers

Scripture passage

> Then Peter came and said to [Jesus], 'Lord, if another mem-
> ber of the church sins against me, how often should I forgive?
> As many as seven times?' Jesus said to him, 'Not seven times,
> but, I tell you, seventy-seven times.'
> (Mt 18:21-22)

Reflection

This incident is coloured by Matthew's concern for unity in the
diverse early church community over which he presided – pos-
sibly at Antioch. Hence, his designation of 'another member of
the church' is more pastorally fitting than the usual generic
translation of 'my brother'. Peter's question to Jesus, as Matthew
words it, is: How often should I forgive an offending fellow
member of the church community? Peter himself suggests –
very generously he thinks – seven times but our Lord says seventy-seven times, or seventy times seven. The Greek text allows
for either translation. Seventy-seven times is not intended to be
taken literally. It means, without limit or as often as required.

Are we then expected to forgive our offending brother and
sister in the church community over and over again, almost
mindlessly? There is no question here of the repeated forgiveness of one who is not truly repentant, or of allowing ourselves
to be the proverbial doormat for another. Nor is there question
of aiding and abetting the callous repeat offender. The point is
that fellow members of the church should be forgiven when
they are truly contrite, even if through genuine weakness they
offend again and again.

The scholar John P. Meier sees Jesus' expansive teaching on
forgiveness as 'a reversal of the cry for excessive vengeance' by
Lamach (a descendant of Cain who killed Abel) which is found
in the Bible's record of the early years of the human race.
'Lamach said to his wives: "Adah and Zillah ... listen to what I

say. I have killed a man for wounding me, a young man for striking me. If Cain is avenged sevenfold, truly Lamach is avenged seventy-seven fold".' (Gen 4:23-24) Jesus may have had this scripture in mind – and a tradition of vengeance rather than forgiveness – when he spoke his new expansive teaching on forgiveness. It reverses Lamach's vengeance, even to the mention of 'sevenfold' and 'seventy-seven fold'. It is a teaching foreign to the biblical past, and even to our own natural instinct of fair play, and yet we cannot imagine a lesser teaching coming from a heart as understanding as Christ's. The quality of forgiveness he desires from all such as ourselves who want to be his true followers is one which Meier calls 'measureless mercy' and 'forgiveness without frontiers.' (*New Testament Message: Matthew*)

If we are tempted to balk at all of this, let us remember that our repeated forgiveness of the other is based on a combination of their contriteness yet weakness. And we must tell ourselves that our repeated forgiveness of another hardly exceeds in number the times that our heavenly Father repeats his mercy and forgiveness with respect to ourselves.

Prayer
Forgiving Father: Grant me patience and perseverance in forgiving repeatedly the one who continues to insult or injure me. I do not ask to understand why that person does not change once and for all. Instead, point me to my own weaknesses and repeated failings, and to your repeated absolution of them. And remind me of the insight of the Little Flower, so sensitive to sin herself and yet so understanding of our weak nature, who said that there are souls for whom your mercy never tires of waiting, souls to whom you grant your light only by degrees. Amen.

Wednesday of the third week of Lent

Lessening Our Losses

Scripture passage

> See, just as the Lord my God has charged me, I now teach
> you statutes and ordinances for you to observe in the land
> that you are about to enter and occupy. You must observe
> them diligently, for this will show your wisdom and discern-
> ment to the peoples, who, when they hear all these statutes,
> will say, 'Surely this great nation is a wise and discerning
> people!' ... But take care and watch yourselves closely, so as
> neither to forget the things that your eyes have seen nor to let
> them slip from your mind all the days of your life; make
> them known to your children and your children's children.
> (Deut 4:5-9)

Reflection

This scripture passage is part of Moses' exhortation to the
Israelites, on the east side of the Jordan river, as they prepare to
enter the Promised Land. Since the Canaanites still live in the
land, Moses warns the Israelites against the false gods and the
graven images of Canaan which they will encounter. He charges
them to maintain their identity as God's chosen people, with
obedience to God's law and loyalty to him. All of this is critical if
they are to survive and prosper in the land 'which I swore to
Abraham, to Isaac, and to Jacob.' (Deut 34:4)

If Moses' exhortation is to be effective, he realises that some
catechesis is called for! He needs to review the law of God, its
statutes and its ordinances for the benefit of the people. And this
he does in great detail (as found in various passages of
Deuteronomy). One could call Moses' exhortation – several exhortations in fact – a catechism. Moses also knows that religious
knowledge is only half of the battle in religious education; moti-
vation is the other half! So he tells God's people that by living up
to the law, its statutes and ordinances they will save themselves
from all the sorts of trouble that torment people who lack God

and his guidance. In addition, others will look at God's people in admiration and say that they are a great people, so wise and discerning. And God, of course, will continue to bless them and they will prosper in the land. All of this depends on their living by God's law, statutes and ordinances. These, therefore, must not be allowed to 'slip from your mind' and 'you must make them known to your children and your children's children.'

We present-day believers should read ourselves into this scripture passage and accept its catechetical challenges for our own time and place. The world around us, at variance with faith and with God's law, is the land of Canaan in modern garb. It has its own pantheon of false gods and graven images of which we must beware. Moses challenges us to maintain our faith and uphold our standards in our neo-pagan ethos. But we will not do so successfully unless great numbers of us amend our religious ignorance of even the basics of our Christian faith. Nor will we do it successfully until others of us stop being the faces that show up in the major exposés and inquiries and tribunals that depress everyone's spirit. For so much of what has been going wrong in our society, we may not point the finger only at the malinfluence of 'the big, bad world' of modern Canaan but at our own less than well-instructed and well-motivated selves too.

Prayer

Dear Holy Spirit: Consoler of the church! Advocate of the gospel! We are at a crossroads. The church is irrelevant to many lives. The gospel is not known to a multitude in the so-called Christian West. People are perplexed by God's seeming absence from the world and its tragedies. Those of us with faith are on the firing line, without answers that satisfy. Even the heroic life of the saint is viewed by some as no more than one manner of living, among other and equal variables. Come, then, fill our hearts with your wisdom! Renew the face of the earth! Amen.

Thursday of the third week of Lent

About Neutrality

Scripture passage

> [Jesus] knew what they were thinking and said to them,
> 'Every kingdom divided against itself becomes a desert, and
> a house divided collapses ... Whoever is not with me is
> against me, and whoever does not gather with me scatters.'
> (Lk 11:17,23)

Reflection

We hear calls from time to time for a public debate on the issue
of Ireland and neutrality. Our constitution does not establish
our neutrality, and our so-called neutrality during the Second
World War was little more than a matter of hastily declaring
ourselves a non-belligerent. Even so, we were, as the saying
goes, neutral in favour of one side. For example, I remember the
B-17 bomber that crash-landed in the grounds of the agricultural
college in Athenry in 1943. It was hopelessly off-course. Its occu-
pants included several US Generals involved in planning the D-
Day invasion. My father was a Garda at the scene, and I knew
that the Americans were whisked up to the Border that night
under cover of darkness. I also knew that if they had been
Germans they would have been whisked up to the POW camp
in the Curragh.

Jesus raises the issue of neutrality in our scripture passage,
but in the more acute context of the great moral struggle between himself and Satan for the soul of humankind and each of
us. In our scripture passage, Jesus is speaking to the Pharisees,
trying to convince them that the kingdom of God, not that of
Satan, is being manifested in him through his power to expel
demons. They must therefore side with him, else they are
against him. They cannot be neutral about him and his mission.

Regarding ourselves, we may say that the Lord is equally
sure that we of this generation, as the inheritors of the faith and

of his saving way, cannot be neutral today. Nor can we have one foot in his kingdom and the other in the un-graced world, hedging our bets. We cannot be divided about Jesus or divided in our commitment to his way. For a kingdom divided only falls, he says, and a house divided only collapses upon itself. And elsewhere, of course, he warned of the impossibility of serving two masters, such service being understood in its traditional sense of full-time duty and undivided loyalty.

Prayer
Lord Jesus: My prayer is for all of us who do our best to follow you. When we hear of unity, may we think primarily of the unity of our mind and heart with yours. When we hear of fidelity, may we think primarily of fidelity to your word in its uniqueness and in its integrity. When we name our ethical priorities, may they be the ones you name in the gospels. Protect us from redirecting your word and your priorities onto the path of our own so that they are changed or muted. Fill us with reverence for your divine word, allowing it its full freedom and integrity. May we live by your word as faithfully as possible so that we are always confident about being with you and not against you, of gathering with you and never scattering. Amen.

Friday of the third week of Lent

Conversion

Scripture passage

> Return, O Israel to the Lord your God, for you have collapsed
> because of your iniquity. Take words with you and return to
> the Lord; say to him, 'Take away all guilt; accept that which
> is good, and we will offer the fruit of our lips. Assyria shall
> not save us; we will not ride upon horses; we will say no
> more, "Our god," to the work of our hands. In you the or-
> phan finds mercy' ... Those who are wise understand these
> things; those who are discerning know them. For the ways of
> the Lord are right, and the upright walk in them, but trans-
> gressors stumble in them.
> (Hos 14:2-4, 10)

Reflection

Hosea is listed among the so-called minor prophets. He is a re-
markable prophet nonetheless. He lived in the eighth century
before Christ. He was married to a woman named Gomer and
she was unfaithful to him. She had a wandering heart and was
involved in several liaisons. Scripture scholars suggest that
Hosea's second and third children were born of such affairs, and
that Hosea was painfully aware of this. But he was never vindic-
tive. On the contrary, he loved Gomer all the more.

His real-life experience with Gomer and his re-action to her
infidelity inform his view of God's people as the unfaithful wife
and God himself as the ever-loving, forgiving husband. God
and his people are in a sacred marriage sealed by a covenant. So
Hosea addresses Israel and tells her that her infidelity has
caused her collapse. The collapse is not just on the moral level,
but on all levels including the political, economic and psycho-
logical. He pulls no punches. He says flatly, 'You have collapsed
through your guilt.'

He then calls Israel to a conversion of heart. She must return
to her Lord with words of repentance and ask him to 'forgive all

iniquity.' She must tell her Lord that she will no more look to pagan Assyria for safety or rely on 'horses to mount.' 'Horses to mount' is perhaps a reference to the cavalry of the Egyptians. Israel must tell her Lord that she will not turn again to false gods and graven images and admit that these are nothing more than 'the work of our hands'. Israel is, in effect, now orphaned on all levels because of her infidelity. Her experiences with people of power, with human alliances, with man-made gods and hollow images have brought her to the stage where she has nothing and can depend only on her compassionate, forgiving, loving and ever-faithful God.

Prayer

My dearest Father: How often have I not 'collapsed because of [my] iniquity'! How often have I not said 'my God' to the work of my hands, and put myself at the centre of my universe, and wished to put myself at the centre of everyone else's universe too! Hosea is experienced and insightful in his religious psychology: the sin of the believer has consequences that the sin of the unbeliever does not have. It is the one trained in your ways, dearest Father, who is the one that 'stumbles' with guilt and remorse while the untrained unbeliever remains unmoved in the 'innocence' of his ignorance. Save me then, dearest Father, from every serious sin. Deliver me so that I do not 'collapse in iniquity' or 'stumble' under the weight of guilt and remorse. I make my fervent prayer through Christ our Lord. Amen.

Saturday of the third week of Lent

An Offer Refused

Scripture passage

> A certain ruler asked him, 'Good Teacher, what must I do to inherit eternal life?' Jesus said to him, 'You know the commandments ...' He replied, 'I have kept all these since my youth.' When Jesus heard this, he said to him, 'There is still one thing lacking. Sell all that you own and distribute the money to the poor, and you will have treasure in heaven; then come, follow me.' But when he heard this, he became sad; for he was very rich. Jesus looked at him and said, 'How hard it is for those who have wealth to enter the kingdom of God!'
> (Lk 18:18-24)

Reflection

Why did this ruler among the Jews ask Jesus what he must do to inherit eternal life? As a pious Jew, he already knew the answer: keep the commandments of God. And he knew that Jesus would most likely give the same answer. Keeping the commandments was the heart of the Law and this led to eternal life. Was the ruler, then, sincere in asking his question? Or was he testing Jesus, perhaps hoping to get a controversial reply and so create difficulty for Jesus and notoriety for himself? Or had he set up this scene so that he could trumpet his holiness in public? – 'I have kept all these since my youth!'

Let us give the man the benefit of the doubt. We may assume that he was searching for something more than usual – maybe greater sacrifice, or a deeper spirituality, or perfection – and that he sensed that Jesus might be the one to direct him. At any rate, Jesus suggests one more step that the ruler might take. It is not a step necessary for friendship with God or for normal access to heaven, but to have what Jesus calls added 'treasure' there. He says, 'Sell all that you own ... distribute the money to the poor ... then come, follow me.' Jesus likely offered this invitation to the ruler because he saw the potential for spiritual greatness in the man. But it was a bridge too far for him. 'When he heard this, he became sad; for he was very rich.' Jesus said, 'How hard it is for those who have wealth to enter the kingdom of God!' Why did Jesus say that?

If we look at our history books, or take note of our inquiries and tribunals, we know why Jesus said what he said. We know because we see people undone by their riches and by their craving for money. We see lives gone astray, careers blighted, and families humiliated because of the worship of money. We see ideals surrendered, judgements compromised, associates betrayed, and the high moral ground not held. Such behaviour contradicts the gospel of the kingdom of God and prevents the conduct of a life or a business in line with the gospel. Hence, Jesus rightly notes that it is hard for the rich to enter the kingdom. But he did not say it is impossible. It is never impossible for anyone with goodwill and grace to be governed by the gospel and committed to our Lord's wide-hearted values.

Prayer

I must ask you, dearest Father, to destroy the greed that grips many hearts in our prosperous economy. It is said that we are ripping-off each other in our scramble for profit, acquisition and wealth. What does this say about us in terms of who we are becoming and what we really believe? Is it all an indicator of shallow faith? I prayed long ago that our people would experience a little prosperity after their centuries of poverty. Now we have this tidal wave of money and we don't know how to handle it in Christian terms. The best in us is drowning! So, I pray again to you: please grant us balance. Kindly rid us of the covetous heart. May the memory of our impoverished ancestors, and our tradition of the soft heart, and our generosity to every good cause survive this present onslaught and be our saving grace. Amen.

Fourth Sunday of Lent

Lifted Up For Us

Scripture passage

> [Jesus said], 'And just as Moses lifted up the serpent in the wilderness, so must the Son of Man be lifted up, that whoever believes in him may have eternal life. For God so loved the world that he gave his only Son, so that everyone who believes in him may not perish but may have eternal life.'
> (Jn 3:14-16)

Reflection

God invites the world he so loves to look for salvation. The world so loved by God is the world of people, the world of great and small people, the world of good and flawed people. God loves intensely this whole world of humanity simply because he is its Father and they are his children. He is bound to them by love.

Salvation is easily found. And Jesus tells humanity where to find it. Look up, he says, and see God's beloved Son lifted up on his cross, and look up again and see him lifted up in glory. This double lifting-up of God's beloved Son makes salvation possible for every human being who wishes to look up at the face of Jesus with faith and love.

Jesus uses a familiar image to make his point. During their exodus journey, the people of Israel wandered in the wilderness of what is known to us today as the Sinai Peninsula where the modern Israelis and Egyptians have fought their recent wars. The people lost confidence in God and they hankered for the safety (and the bondage!) of Egypt. Their punishment for their loss of confidence in God's guidance was a plague of deadly serpents. But God told Moses to make a molten image of a serpent and lift it up over the people. Anyone who looked at it in faith and trust would live. The uplifted brazen serpent was the instrument of God's healing in the physical sense. Jesus lifted up on his cross and in glory is the instrument of God's healing of the whole person, body and spirit and soul. Coming near the end of his life on earth, Jesus said, 'When I am lifted up from the earth, I will draw all people to myself.' (Jn 12:32)

We have many distractions these days. And we have new religions held up before our faces looking for our attention. And, as usual, we have people who would like to limit salvation according to the narrowness of their theology and the smallness of their hearts. It seems helpful then to remind ourselves and others that God 'desires everyone to be saved and to come to the knowledge of the truth.' (1 Tim 2:4) And it is helpful to tell ourselves and others, again and again, that the deed of salvation was done for us in Christ and in no one and nothing else. Eternal life is here for any and all who lift up their eyes to the Lord Jesus and allow him to draw them to himself.

Prayer
Sacred Heart of Jesus: Draw all souls to yourself. Draw those of weak faith and of no faith. Draw those who have fallen away, and those whose faith is weak, and those who are perplexed by the violence of nature and the violence of man, and those dispirited by the church's inconsistencies and their own. Draw myself, and those I love, and those for whom I am in any way responsible. Allow all of us to see your cross and your glory beckoning us, covering all our concerns, absolving our sins, affirming our hope, and pointing our future. May all of us be drawn into the love of your heart so that we may love our good and gracious God with a measure of your burning love for him and for us. Sacred Heart of Jesus, I place all my trust in you. Amen.

Activity for the fourth week of Lent
Many of our crosses are self-inflicted. Try to identify a self-inflicted cross whose removal would free your mind, soul and spirit, especially a cross fashioned from carelessness, compulsion or self-indulgence. Make this week the first week of your determination to be rid of it.

Monday of the fourth week of Lent

From a Distance

Scripture passage

Now there was a royal official whose son lay ill in Capernaum. When he heard that Jesus had come from Judea to Galilee, he went and begged him to come down and heal his son, for he was at the point of death. Then Jesus said to him, 'Unless you see signs and wonders you will not believe.' The official said to him, 'Sir, come down before my little boy dies.' Jesus said to him, 'Go; your son will live.' The man believed the word that Jesus spoke to him and started on his way. As he was going down, his slaves met him and told him that his child was alive. So he asked them the hour when he began to recover, and they said to him, 'Yesterday at one in the afternoon the fever left him.' The father realised that this was the hour when Jesus had said to him, 'Your son will live.' So he himself believed, along with his whole household.
(Jn 4:46-53)

Reflection

The exchange between Jesus and this royal official takes place in Nazareth about twenty miles north of Capernaum. The royal official is likely a member of the court of King Herod. In response to the official's request on behalf of his dying son, Jesus' initial reaction seems out of place. He says, 'Unless you see signs and wonders you will not believe.' The scholars suggest that Jesus – and perhaps our gospel writer John – is addressing a wider audience than the single official himself. He is addressing the Jews. He is rebuking them, and any of us now, who put signs and wonders ahead of faith and trust in Jesus. And there is a caution here for some of us today who tend to rush to every new message and miracle rather than to the enduring word of God.

Time and again in the gospels, Jesus responds positively to requests which are grounded in the virtue of faith, and specifically grounded in trust in him. How often have we not heard

Jesus say such lines as, 'Your faith has saved you' (Lk 7:50) and 'Go your way; your faith has made you whole' (Lk 17:19)? We notice that the royal official twice asks Jesus to come down from Nazareth to Capernaum to heal his son. This repetition of his request does not reflect a lack of faith. We may assume that the repeated 'come down' only reflects the common experience of healing in which the healer and the healed are in each other's presence.

When Jesus says, 'Go; your son will live,' the official believes unquestioningly. He now knows – and so do we – that Jesus does not need to be physically in the other's presence in order to heal. Jesus can heal from a distance.

Prayer

Dearest Jesus: I trust you completely. I thank you for your magnificent life, your magnificent words, your magnificent graces. I know that you answer the prayer of the one who trusts in you. Long ago you healed the trusting official's child. You even healed the child 'from a distance'. Distance did not matter to your heart or to your healing ability. Nor does it matter between you and me, except it be the distance which I may put between us by my lack of trust. Save me then, dearest Jesus, from the distance that I alone may create: the distance of a weaker trust, a poorer love, a lesser ardour, a blurred focus. Amen.

Tuesday of the fourth week of Lent

Healing Us

Scripture passage

After this there was a festival of the Jews, and Jesus went up to Jerusalem. Now in Jerusalem by the Sheep Gate there is a pool, called in Hebrew Bethzatha, which has five porticoes. In these lay many invalids – blind, lame, and paralysed. One man was there who had been ill for thirty-eight years. When Jesus saw him lying there and knew that he had been there a long time, he said to him, 'Do you want to be made well?' The sick man answered him, 'Sir, I have no one to put me into the pool when the water is stirred up; and while I am making my way, someone else steps down ahead of me.' Jesus said to him, 'Stand up, take your mat and walk.' At once the man was made well, and he took up his mat and began to walk. Now that day was a sabbath. So the Jews said to the man who had been cured, 'It is the sabbath; it is not lawful for you to carry your mat.' But he answered them, 'The man who made me well said to me, "Take up your mat and walk".' ... Therefore the Jews started persecuting Jesus, because he was doing such things on the sabbath.
(Jn 5:1-16)

Reflection

The pool by the Sheep Gate is better known to us as Bethsaida or Bethesda. Those who were ill gathered there in hope of a cure. The pool was believed to cure the first one into it when the water was 'stirred up.' This happened only very occasionally. The stirring may have been due to the activity of a spasmodic spring which had some curative properties or, as popularly believed, to the action of an angel of the Lord.

The sick man explains to Jesus that he has failed in thirty-eight years to get into the pool at the stirring of the water. His illness makes him too slow. Perhaps the years of waiting have further atrophied him. 'While I am making my way,' he says, 'someone else steps down ahead of me.' It may seem strange to us that nobody has helped this man into the pool in thirty-eight years. Perhaps no one helped him because it would amount to favouritism and give him an edge over the equally ill others. Or perhaps, as scholar William Barclay notes, he may be accustomed to his condition and a cure would force him into something entirely novel – work to make a living! Maybe this is why Jesus asks him very pointedly, 'Do you [really] want to be made well?' When our Lord is satisfied that he does, he makes him well.

Some Jews object to the man's cure because it occurs on the sabbath and criticise him for carrying his mat (i.e. his bed) about on the sabbath. And they turn on Jesus: 'The Jews started persecuting Jesus because he was doing such things on the sabbath.'

Since John, our gospel writer, is a theologian of sign and symbol, it is likely that he sees this incident in a Messianic light. In this light, the sick man and those who languish by the sheep pool may be viewed as God's flock waiting for their Shepherd. The five porticoes at the sheep pool which shade them from the burning sun while they wait are the five books of the Law, i.e. the Torah. The Law helps them but does not heal them. The thirty-eight years of waiting may symbolise the (presumed) number of centuries that fallen man has waited for his Saviour. And, in John's eyes, the stirring of the water may stand for the curative power of baptism. William Barclay notes that the art of the early Christian church often depicts 'a man rising from the baptismal waters carrying a bed on his back.' (*Daily Study Bible: John*)

Prayer

Lord Jesus: I come before you for healing. Lift the sins I carry on my back. Lift my grief over opportunities missed and paths not taken. Lighten the load of my life's mixed history. Allow the Spirit to stir the healing waters in my regard. Direct me to those healing waters of quiet communion with you, of word of scripture and grace of sacrament. Amen.

Wednesday of the fourth week of Lent

Declaring His Authority

Scripture passage

[Jesus said], 'Very truly, I tell you, anyone who hears my word and believes him who sent me has eternal life, and does not come under judgement, but has passed from death to life. Very truly, I tell you, the hour is coming, and is now here, when the dead will hear the voice of the Son of God, and those who hear will live. For just as the Father has life in himself, so he has granted the Son also to have life in himself; and he has given him authority to execute judgement, because he is the Son of Man. Do not be astonished at this; for the hour is coming when all who are in their graves will hear his voice and will come out – those who have done good, to the resurrection of life, and those who have done evil, to the resurrection of condemnation.'

(Jn 5:24-29)

Reflection

The background to this passage is Jesus' breaking of the sabbath with such good deeds as the cure of the sick man at the pool of Bethesda. The leading Jews are angered over his activity and at his independence of the law – and of their authority! As we saw in yesterday's scripture passage, 'they started persecuting Jesus.' (Jn 5:16)

What Jesus says in today's passage goes much, much further: it shocks them. Jesus names himself as Son of God in an exclusive sense. He works good deeds even on the sabbath because 'my Father is still working.' (v. 17) He does not rest from his saving work on the sabbath because the Father doesn't. He gives people life all the time because his Father is life-giving. And as his Father judges, so does he. Jesus underlines the unity of Father and Son and his total obedience to, and expression of, his Father's mind and will. Clearly, he stands on one side of a great theological divide and his caustic critics on the other. He is also very forthright in what he says, and thereby gives his enemies grounds for his later condemnation on the charge of blasphemy.

Jesus says that the Father has given him 'the authority to execute judgement.' Judgement will be executed in the 'hour that is coming', viz. the Day of Judgement. Harsh or benign judgement depends on whether people 'hear his voice' or ignore it. Some elect to hear it, others choose to ignore it. There is the echo here of the words of the prophet Simeon at the Lord's presentation in the temple: 'This child is destined for the fall and the rise of many in Israel.' (Lk 2:14) Those of us, then, who are captivated by Jesus and captured by his word have little to fear at his coming to execute judgement. For we do not 'come under judgement' as such, having already 'passed from death to life' through our fellowship with him.

Prayer

Lord Jesus: I pray this day for all in positions of authority in church and state. Theirs is a very challenging and highly accountable trust. Help them to carry out their duties well, and to find fulfilment in work well done. Divest them of the natural tendency to exaggerate their authority and inflate their self-importance, as did the leaders of Israel in their confrontations with you. Let them know that no one is irreplaceable in life or in ministry, and that their office is a trust for which they must render an account not only to history but, as you say in our scripture passage, on the Day of Judgement, in 'the hour that is coming.' Amen.

Thursday of the fourth week of Lent

The Crucial Voice

Scripture passage

[Jesus said], 'The Father who sent me has himself testified on my behalf. You have never heard his voice or seen his form, and you do not have his word abiding in you, because you do not believe him whom he has sent.You search the scriptures because you think that in them you have eternal life; and it is they that testify on my behalf. Yet you refuse to come to me to have life. I do not accept glory from human beings. But I know that you do not have the love of God in you. I have come in my Father's name, and you do not accept me; if another comes in his own name, you will accept him.'
(Jn 5:37-43)

Reflection

Our Lord continues to make his case for healing the sick on the sabbath, and indeed for his authority over the sabbath. He continues to identify the reasons why he and the Father are one in mind and will. And he rounds on the critics who refuse to listen to him. The Lord sees his voice as the most crucial voice in our listening lives, the consummate word that God speaks to men and women in their life's passage. Not to hear his voice is the tragedy of all tragedies.

You do not have God's word abiding in you, says Jesus to his critics, because you do not listen to me who am the consummate word of God! You search the scriptures looking for eternal life, and you cannot see that the scriptures point you to me! You cherish Moses and the Law but you refuse to see me as their fulfilment! We may wish to remind ourselves that we can be expert in the study of the scriptures and yet be without conviction or even conversion. And we may wish to tell ourselves to stop chasing after sundry 'messages' because the only message God wants us to hear is found in its fullness in Jesus and his gospel.

Jesus says, 'I have come in my Father's name, and you do not accept me; if another comes in his own name, you will accept him.' Jesus' assertion is not far-fetched. The history of his people is replete with would-be Messiahs and revolutionaries, all of whom had their quota of devoted followers. Even at the end of his life Jesus has to compete with another political revolutionary, Barabbas, for the favour of the people. And we know who the people chose.

In every generation, Jesus competes with others for a hearing. In our generation, the competition is intense, almost off the map entirely because of the sheer quantity of the media of communication and the variety of the voices. Fibre optic, wire, line, mobile, monitor, screen and satellite are filled with 'the good, the bad and the ugly'. The 'good' include the voices that are beneficial to our education, our health and general welfare. But included in the 'good', and foremost among the good for us, has to be the voice we need to hear more than any other, the voice of Jesus.

Prayer
Lord Jesus: My world and my days are full of voices. They compete for my time and attention. They look for my love and loyalty. Many of these are healing voices, responding to my needs in friendship, education, health and culture. Some are the entreating voices that come with vocation, service or spontaneous need. Others are damaging voices, or empty and distracting voices. There is one voice I attend to for the sure direction of my life, for its deeper meaning, for inner peace and the promise of the future. It is your voice, dearest Jesus. May you always speak to me through scripture and in prayer; and may I never lose my love of listening to the surest, most fulfilling and dearest voice I know. Thank you. Amen.

Friday of the fourth week of Lent

Remaining Righteous

Scripture passage

'Let us lie in wait for the righteous man,
because he is inconvenient to us and opposes our actions;
he reproaches us for sins against the law,
and accuses us of sins against our training.
He professes to have knowledge of God,
and calls himself a child of the Lord.
He became to us a reproof of our thoughts;
the very sight of him is a burden to us,
because his manner of life is unlike that of others,
and his ways are strange.
Let us test him ...'
(Wis 2:12-15, 19)

Reflection

The book of Wisdom may be viewed as promotional literature. It advocates the life of faith. It was likely composed to encourage Jewish believers whose faith had weakened under the oppression of paganism and the malice of apostate Jews. Its rallying cry is: Love justice and pursue it! Love wisdom and pursue it! The first upholds the lifestyle of the righteous or just person. The second advocates loyalty to God by following his ways.

The author of the book of Wisdom is not the wise King Solomon, but he often speaks his words as though Solomon himself were speaking. This adds weight to the author's pastoral exhortations. I suppose that, like all good prophets and pastors, he is trying to encourage faith as best he can in the midst of life's challenges and in the particular circumstances of his own time and place.

The pastoral task before him is the same, in some ways, as that facing pastors today. The people's faith needs supporting as the Greek 'scientific' viewpoint, free thought, pagan religion and the worship of idols lay siege to it. In this 'scientific' and pagan setting, good is being called evil and evil good, and life beyond death is denied. The book of Wisdom contends with all of this by celebrating the truth, value and nobility of the faith. In the face of the denial of life beyond death, for example, Wisdom crafts the theological sentiments and the sentences of hope which we still use in our Christian funeral liturgy today: 'The souls of the righteous [the just] are in the hand of God, and no torment will ever touch them. In the eyes of the foolish they seemed to have died, and their departure was thought to be a disaster, and their going from us to be their destruction, but they are at peace ... Their hope is full of immortality.' (Wis 3:1-4)

Like the righteous or just person in our scripture passage, the individual believer today (and the church as a whole) is being observed critically. And the lines spoken by the unbeliever and the former believer roughly twenty-one hundred years ago in our scripture passage are spoken again today. They may not be spoken in the exact same manner, or with the same degree of malice, but they are spoken and we should be challenged by that fact. 'Let us lie in wait for the righteous man ... He professes to have knowledge of God ... and calls himself a child of God ... His manner of life is unlike that of others ... Let us test him.' We should not run away from this challenge, much less condemn it. We should face it. The Lord is our support.

Prayer
May God support us all the day long, till the shadows lengthen, and the evening comes, and the busy world is hushed, and the fever of life is over, and our work is done. Then, in his mercy, may he give us a safe lodging and a holy rest, and peace at the last. Amen. (*Cardinal Newman*)

Saturday of the fourth week of Lent

Amazing Grace

Scripture passage

On the last day of the festival, the great day, while Jesus was standing there, he cried out, 'Let anyone who is thirsty come to me, and let the one who believes in me drink. As the scripture has said, "Out of the believer's heart shall flow rivers of living water".' Now he said this about the Spirit, which believers in him were to receive; for as yet there was no Spirit, because Jesus was not yet glorified. When they heard these words, some in the crowd said, 'This is really the prophet.' Others said, 'This is the Messiah.' But some asked, 'Surely the Messiah does not come from Galilee, does he? Has not the scripture said that the Messiah is descended from David and comes from Bethlehem, the village where David lived? ' So there was a division in the crowd because of him.
(Jn 7:37-43)

Reflection

Each day of the eight-day Festival of Tabernacles there was a water ceremony at the altar of the temple. Water was carried by a priest from the pool of Siloam while the people chanted, 'With joy you will draw water from the wells of salvation.' (Isa 12:3) This water was poured into a perforated bowl on the altar and it flowed over the altar. In this context, Jesus cries out, 'Let anyone who is thirsty come to me, and let the one who believes in me drink. As the scripture has said, "Out of the believer's heart shall flow rivers of living water".' (vv. 37-38)

It is not clear whether 'the believer' is Jesus himself or the one 'who is thirsty' who comes to him. In any event Jesus declares himself to be the source of the water of new life and abounding grace. These will flow like 'rivers of living water' on those, and then from those, who come to him. And this will come to pass when his Spirit is unleashed in the great out-pouring of Pentecost. John's comment, 'as yet there was no Spirit' may be taken to mean that until the Pentecost event there had been no mighty activity of the Spirit. Such could occur only after Jesus' glorification.

It is this cry of Jesus, this claim that out of him would flow the living waters that sparks the people's discussion over whether he might be the Messiah. It leads to a 'division in the crowd because of him'. And so, Jesus' offer of amazing grace is missed as the discussion heats up instead over whether Nazareth or Bethlehem is the more fitting birth place for the Messiah.

Prayer

Our Father in heaven: We poor humans so often miss the forest for the trees. We go off on tangents and forget the issue or the invitation. Likewise in this passage, your beloved Son, the promised of the ages with his waters of life-giving grace, is bypassed in a discussion about whether the Messiah should come from Nazareth or from Bethlehem. He comes from you! And he unleashes your Spirit! He offers these parched people, with their desert history, the waters of life and they lose his invitation in a discussion about two names on a map! But I thank you, dear Father, and all Christian believers thank you for the Amazing Grace you send to set us free. Glory then to you, Father, and to your beloved Son, and to the Holy Spirit now and forever. Amen.

Fifth Sunday of Lent

The Hour

Scripture passage

[Jesus said], 'The hour has come for the Son of Man to be glorified. Very truly, I tell you, unless a grain of wheat falls into the earth and dies, it remains just a single grain; but if it dies, it bears much fruit. Those who love their life lose it, and those who hate their life in this world will keep it for eternal life. Whoever serves me must follow me, and where I am, there will my servant be also. Whoever serves me, the Father will honour.Now my soul is troubled. And what should I say – 'Father, save me from this hour'? No, it is for this reason that I have come to this hour. Father, glorify your name.' Then a voice came from heaven, 'I have glorified it, and I will glorify it again.'

(Jn 12:23-28)

Reflection

Jesus identifies himself as the Son of Man and announces that the hour has come for him to be glorified. How would his hearers back then have understood his words? They would have assumed that he was identifying himself as the ideal king of Israel, long promised by their God, a king in the style of such predecessor-heroes as the Judges, Samuel, David and Judas Maccabeus (the 'Hammer'), and as the great king who would now liberate them from the Romans and begin Israel's reign of power and prosperity. For them, 'the hour' is the arrival of this new and glorious kingdom. But they are mistaken because they are thinking mainly in a political context.

The kingdom of Jesus is not of this world (in the political sense) and 'the hour' is the start of that sequence of saving events which we have come to call the paschal mystery. And the glory to be bestowed on Jesus by the Father is not an earthly glory but the glory due a beloved and obedient Son, the Servant of God and the Saviour of all humanity.

The sequence of saving events begins with our Lord's betrayal and condemnation; it moves through the stages of his passion and death; and on to his resurrection and glorification. Jesus says of himself, 'Unless a grain of wheat falls into the earth and dies, it remains just a single grain; but if it dies, it bears much fruit.' Unless he undergoes death and burial he cannot rise in new life as pleasing harvest. Jesus invites his disciples to hear and to accept what for them is a novel and a radical understanding of the promised kingdom and the promised glory. Of course, he invites you and me to hear and to accept the same.

His words about the grain of wheat dying and being transformed has application to our lives as well as to his. Jesus invites us to believe that true life or real living here on earth is life lived for, and surrendered to, the service of others. He says, 'Those who hate their life in this world will keep it for eternal life.' He means that we should invest our lives in the lives and on the salutary concerns of others. It is only by dying to the priorities of the self and of the world, and surrendering our lives to the needs of others, that much fruit will spring from the single grain that each believer is. And as the others-serving life of Jesus ends in the glory of the Father's presence, so will our others-serving lives end. For Jesus made this promise: 'Where I am, there will my servant be also.' (Jn 12:26)

Prayer

Jesus: You had such an intense appreciation of your 'hour' in ministry and service. You worked without concern for yourself, only conscious of your Father's will and the needs of our salvation. The hour of your ministry and service led inflexibly to the hour of your glorification. Allow me to make good use of my hour here on earth, whether I be priest or lay person, single or married, young or elderly, multi-talented or modestly blessed. None of that really matters so long as I live my hour as best I can and reach that other hour which is my resurrection and glory in your presence forever. Amen.

Activity for the fifth week of Lent
Attend the Parish Penitential Service. If this is held some other week, substitute that week's activity for this week's.

Monday of the fifth week of Lent

Not Judging Others

Scripture passage

Early in the morning [Jesus] came again to the temple. All the people came to him and he sat down and began to teach them. The scribes and the Pharisees brought a woman who had been caught in adultery; and making her stand before all of them, they said to him, 'Teacher, this woman was caught in the very act of committing adultery. Now in the law Moses commanded us to stone such women. Now what do you say?' They said this to test him, so that they might have some charge to bring against him. Jesus bent down and wrote with his finger on the ground. When they kept on questioning him, he straightened up and said to them, 'Let anyone among you who is without sin be the first to throw a stone at her.' And once again he bent down and wrote on the ground. When they heard it, they went away, one by one, beginning with the elders; and Jesus was left alone with the woman standing before him. Jesus straightened up and said to her, 'Woman, where are they? Has no one condemned you?' She said, 'No one, sir.' And Jesus said, 'Neither do I condemn you. Go your way, and from now on do not sin again.' (Jn 8:2-11)

Reflection

This is one of the incidents in which Christ most touches our human heart. We see his awareness of the woman's deadly situation before the law and in the face of a crowd ready for blood. We see his sensitivity to the woman's human rights and dignity. To him these count for more than Moses' law. Then we see how the seemingly random doodling of Jesus' finger in the dust and his single line, 'Let anyone among you who is sinless cast the first stone,' deflates the self-righteousness of the woman's accusers and diffuses the explosive situation. And we see the compassion of Christ for a lone individual, and are made to wonder about the quality of our own.If the need for a review of the quality of our compassion is one lesson we may draw from this scene, the danger in judging people is another. Our judgement will, all too often, be a false judgement. It is not only a matter of lacking all the facts, and not knowing the motive or the circumstances of another's action, but of ourselves lacking sufficient moral achievement and holiness to set ourselves up as the moral judges of anyone. Perhaps this is why moral judgements are only safe in the mind of the all-knowing, all-holy God. And perhaps it's why Jesus said to his disciples during the Sermon on the Mount, 'Do not judge, so that you may not be judged yourselves.' (Mt 7:1) Life is full of idle rumour, faulty gossip and false judgement. So why add to the heap?

Prayer
Father: I undertake a review of the quality of my compassion today. Guide my review. Encourage me to refrain from subjecting your children to the judgement of my faulty mind and flawed heart. Help me to avoid the fated gossip session which wastes my time without lessening my ignorance. Impress on me, who claim to be your disciple and not a disciple of the ways of this world, the words which your Son spoke to his disciples during the Sermon of the Mount: 'Do not judge, so that you may not be judged yourselves.' So much of our lives is wasted on false judgements and then spent trying to repair the damage. Forgive me my past lapses in understanding and compassion. Bless my review which I undertake today and strengthen my resolve. Direct my future treatment of your children, and remind me that they are my equal sisters and brothers before your face and in your heart. Amen.

Tuesday of the fifth week of Lent

Going His Way

Scripture passage

Again he said to them, 'I am going away, and you will search for me, but you will die in your sin. Where I am going, you cannot come.' Then the Jews said, 'Is he going to kill himself? Is that what he means by saying, "Where I am going you cannot come"?' He said to them, 'You are from below, I am from above; you are of this world, I am not of this world. I told you that you would die in your sins, for you will die in your sins unless you believe that I am he.'

(Jn 8:21-24)

Reflection

As we read John's gospel we are most likely struck by the frequency with which he mentions 'the Jews' in a negative or slighting way. John is the disciple Jesus loved most. 'The Jews' are the adversaries of John's hero, Jesus. And they are blind and stubborn with regard to the Light of God and the Word of God that Jesus is.

So John's gospel is weighted, so to speak, with his passionate commitment to Christ and his sad realisation that Christ has been rejected by the overwhelming majority of his own and John's people. So they become, almost dismissively to him, 'the Jews.' Since John writes long after the Christ event itself, he has had two generations to reflect on the good news of salvation, and this only intensifies for him the calamity that the Jewish rejection of Jesus is. Moreover, the followers of Jesus have, by the time John writes his gospel, been excommunicated by 'the Jews' from the synagogues and they have been formally cursed by at least one convention of rabbis (at Jamnia c. 85 AD). The break of the Jewish Christians (the church) with Judaism is more or less complete by the time John's gospel is finalised. So John has many reasons for frowning upon 'the Jews'!

Jesus tells 'the Jews' that he is going away. He means that he is about to return to his Father. He tells them that after his death they will search for him but not find him, i.e. that they will realise – too late – that he was their way of salvation and the answer to the prayers of all the Jewish generations. They pretend not to understand him, and exclaim derisively, 'Is he going to kill himself?' He concludes that for all their vaunted religious view of themselves they really are 'from below' and 'of this world'. We can react to them by saying, 'How blind they were!' Or we can say, 'How blessed are we who are going his way!' It is the sure way to the Father in heaven.

Prayer

Dear Jesus: The persistent opposition which you encountered from your own people hurt you intensely. We dare to say that we have some appreciation of your pain because we hurt so easily ourselves even over minor matters, and we are quite devastated when our words or plans or hopes are dismissed by those we call 'our own'. I thank you, dearest Jesus, for your endurance in the face of the opposition from 'your own'. I thank you for the three years of being misunderstood, opposed, stonewalled, derided and dismissed by your own people in your effort to save them from themselves. Kindly keep my ears, my mind and my heart always open to your saving words. Amen.

Wednesday of the fifth week of Lent

Truth and Freedom

Scripture passage

Then Jesus said to the Jews who had come to believe in him, 'If you continue in my word, you are truly my disciples; and you will know the truth, and the truth will make you free.' They answered him, 'We are descendants of Abraham and have never been slaves to anyone. What do you mean by saying, "You will be made free"?'
(Jn 8:31-33)

Reflection

Jesus says, 'The truth will make you free.' The American diplomat Herbert Agar wrote, 'The truth that makes men free is for the most part the truth which men prefer not to hear.' (*A Time for Greatness*) The truth that Jesus refers to is the truth of God, with its claim on my mind and heart, but with its attendant salvation.

The truth of God is displayed in the life of Jesus. And it is spoken in his words. It is the truth which frees us from slavery, selfishness and sin. It is the truth which enables us to make good choices and informed decisions. It is the truth by which we enter the kingdom of God so as to light our path on this earth. It is the truth which leads us to eternal life. Jesus says, 'If you continue in my word, you are truly my disciples; and you will know the truth, and the truth will make you free.'

This is simple and straightforward teaching but we humans sometimes succeed in complicating it, shadowing it, drawing all sorts of questionable rules and regulations from it, and even at times forgetting it! In Lent I need to review my relationship with Jesus' word against the backdrop of all the other words which claim my time and my attention. I need to discover for my own good that I am still fully committed to Jesus' word, that I study it as my priority word, and that I do my best to understand it so that I will continue to live in and from this word and enter ever more deeply into the Lord's lovely truth, that truth which alone makes me free.

Prayer

Jesus: I thank you for being the Word of God that became flesh and lived among us. I thank you for your words of spirit and life. I thank you for the stability and the direction that your words give me in a world of many and competing and contradictory words. I thank you because your word is a contesting and a convicting word in the world. I thank you because it is a challenging word in my own life, but also a comforting and a consoling word, a healing and an eternal word. I thank you most of all because it is my saving word. Amen.

Thursday of the fifth week of Lent

Keep His Word!

Scripture passage

[Jesus said], 'Very truly, I tell you, whoever keeps my word will never see death ... Your ancestor Abraham rejoiced that he would see my day; he saw it and was glad.' Then the Jews said to him, 'You are not yet fifty years old, and have you seen Abraham?' Jesus said to them, 'Very truly, I tell you, before Abraham was, I am.' So they picked up stones to throw at him, but Jesus hid himself and went out of the temple. (Jn 8: 51, 56-59)

Reflection

This passage is part of a long disputation between Jesus and his adversaries. He is making the case why his word should be received. The reason is that he comes from God and speaks God's word faithfully. And he has a unique relationship with God. God is his Father in a way God is Father to no one else, and he is God's Son in a unique manner. Therefore, the word he speaks should be accepted as both compelling and complete. The one who hears and keeps it 'will never see death.'

This claim of never seeing death elicits sarcasm from his adversaries. After all, they say, Abraham and the prophets who spoke God's word are dead! Why should they die but not the keeper of Jesus' word? But they misunderstand him. He is speaking of the enduring relationship with God which following his word produces. As Paul writes later, 'I am convinced that neither death, nor life ... nor anything else in all creation will be able to separate us from the love of God in Christ Jesus our Lord.' (Rom 8:38-39)

Jesus says, 'Abraham rejoiced that he would see my day; he saw it and was glad.' The Jews believed that Father Abraham saw all the Jewish days ahead, and particularly the day of the Messiah. So Jesus' statement is his way of stating that he is the Messiah. His adversaries brush the claim aside and, derisively, comment instead on Jesus' youth.

Then follows a truly startling claim by Jesus. He says, 'before Abraham was, I am.' Jesus says in effect that he always existed, as God has always existed. Classical theology refers to this as the pre-existence of Jesus: he is the Word of God made flesh in time. Some scripture scholars suggest it is actually a declaration of the early church which John (much later) attributes to Jesus. At any rate, you and I choose – and have been chosen! – to keep his word so we may not see death.

Prayer
Lord Jesus: You said, 'Before Abraham was, I am.' Your hearers derided you for these words but I gather them to my heart in faith. You existed in the glory of the Godhead before coming among us as our servant and saviour. You put your glory aside and thus emptied yourself to become the slave of our salvation. You became obedient for us 'to the point of death – even death on a cross.' Paul composes a splendid hymn to you and tells us that because of your self-emptying and your saving service God raised you up and exalted you in glory. So now, he says, 'every knee should bend' and 'every tongue should confess' that you are Lord in the glory of the Godhead. (Phil 2:8-11) I bend my heart to your proven lordship and your proven love, dearest Jesus. And so do all who call upon you in faith and follow you with gratitude. Amen.

Friday of the fifth week of Lent

Refusing to Give Way

Scripture passage

> I hear many whispering: 'Terror is all around!
> Denounce him! Let us denounce him!' ...
> But the Lord is with me like a dread warrior;
> therefore my persecutors will stumble, and they will not pre-
> vail ...
> O Lord of hosts, you test the righteous,
> you see the heart and the mind;
> let me see your retribution upon them,
> for to you I have committed my cause.
> Sing to the Lord; praise the Lord!
> For he has delivered the life of the needy
> from the hands of evildoers.
> (Jer 20:10-13)

Reflection

Jeremiah lived in the seventh century before Christ. In many ways, he is a prophet for our time. And his life history is a message for our time. He is called to the prophetic office by God, but deems himself unqualified. He bares his soul to God (and, happily, to us), giving good reasons why God should not choose him for the prophet's work.

Among the reasons is his contemplative rather than active nature. Jeremiah would much prefer a quiet and uncomplicated life! So would most of us! Then there is the fact that an altogether necessary talent for a prophet is the ability to speak well because the prophet speaks for God. But, says Jeremiah, 'I know not how to speak; I am too young.' (Jer 1:6)

Next, Jeremiah senses that his role as a prophet will make him no end of enemies. And he is right! Even his own family will come to plot against him. He will be called upon to condemn the false prophets; to confront, cajole and condemn God's people; to challenge Judah's kings; to be imprisoned himself and endure public disgrace; to watch the destruction of his beloved Jerusalem; live in its ruins; be forced into exile in Egypt and be murdered – most likely by his own.

There are parallels, even some details of similarity, between the life and words and death of Jeremiah and the life and words and death of Jesus. Our scripture passage is one example. There are others in the liturgies of Holy Week. As to ourselves – whether as the church with its recently self-inflicted pain or as a nation with its quietly eroding faith – we read the book of the prophet Jeremiah and find the pathos that wounds our hearts already there wounding his. But even more, we find a severely tested faith, hope and love that simply refuse to give way. Neither should we.

Prayer
Father: Ours is a time of tenuous faith and of lost faith. Many good people are adrift in life, confused as to values, distressed by the demands of work and bills, unsure of your presence, with little hope of a future beyond the grave. Kindly be understanding of them as I know you are. We ourselves, as church, are also in some difficulty. We are perhaps, like the young Jeremiah, reluctant to speak courageously to our time and place. And we seem fearful that our witness may put our feet into the sandals of Jeremiah and make us walk with hostility and in pain. Our faith is no longer supported by the culture which once underpinned it. Some of us mourn the loss. But was such a dependent faith a sufficiently adult faith? Or was it a faith that was too easy and immature, a soft faith set for a fall? Social and cultural change now forces us into a faith that must root itself in your word, gift and grace alone. Bless our desire to be the possessors of the more mature and more pure faith which we believe you are calling forth from us now. We make our prayer through Christ our Lord. Amen.

Saturday of the fifth week of Lent

Blessed Expediency

Scripture passage

The chief priests and the Pharisees called a meeting of the council, and said, 'What are we to do? This man is performing many signs. If we let him go on like this, everyone will believe in him, and the Romans will come and destroy both our holy place and our nation.' But one of them, Caiaphas, who was high priest that year, said to them, 'You know nothing at all! You do not understand that it is better for you to have one man die for the people than to have the whole nation destroyed.' He did not say this on his own, but being high priest that year he prophesied that Jesus was about to die for the nation, and not for the nation only, but to gather into one the dispersed children of God. So from that day on they planned to put him to death.
(Jn 11:47-53)

Reflection

Jesus' raising of Lazarus from the dead, and the awe of the people that went with it, triggered this urgent calling together of the Sanhedrin or priests' council. What, they asked, are we going to do about this Jesus and his miracles; if he continues on his course he will have the whole nation following him and then where will we be? There is no reason to doubt that the Pharisees and especially the priests and Sadducees were chiefly concerned about their own public standing and with keeping power and control firmly in their hands. Jesus had always been a threat to them, and now the threat had become perilous.

The proposition that 'the Romans will come and destroy both our holy place and our nation' is an extreme reaction. The Romans it is true, like all occupying powers, would never tolerate civil disorder, but Jesus was not inciting civil disorder or even mild civil disobedience. (He is the one who said, 'Give to Caesar what is Caesar's.' [Mk 12:17]) The high priest Caiaphas takes control of the gathering and speaks his infamous line, 'It is better to have one man die for the people than to have the whole nation destroyed.' Again, this is extreme talk. It seems to reflect more the threat that Jesus' popularity presents to the priests and leaders than the threat, if any, that his words and miracles could present to Rome.

Caiaphas' infamous line becomes, ironically, a blessing in salvation history. Jesus will indeed die 'for the people' but in a sense that is wholly alien to Caiaphas' social outlook and theological understanding. Jesus will die 'for the people' but the people will turn out to be not just the nation of Israel but the sum total of humanity.

Prayer

Dearest Jesus: Firstly, may I say that I am grateful that the awful, fateful line of Caiaphas became a reality, 'It is better to have one man die for the people than that the whole nation should perish.' Utterly unjust as this sentiment was, it ensured that in selecting you as the one who should die for the sake of the nation your unjust judges ensured your death also for me. I thank you with all my heart for undergoing this both injustice and blessing. Secondly, I ask your forgiveness of all the 'small deaths' I myself have brought to others by my words and actions, my absences and neglects. And thirdly, I ask your forgiveness of church leadership and its lapses over the course of Christian history. In all of these instances, Caiaphas' ethic of expediency was at work however intentionally or unwittingly. Kindly banish from our hearts any intent of victimisation. Banish, too, the attraction of the ethic of expediency whenever justice comes calling with a distressing demand. Amen.

Passion (Palm) Sunday

The Saviour of Israel

Scripture passage

>The next day the great crowd that had come to the festival [of Passover] heard that Jesus was coming to Jerusalem. So they took branches of palm trees and went out to meet him, shouting, 'Hosanna! Blessed is the one who comes in the name of the Lord – the King of Israel!' Jesus found a young donkey and sat on it; as it is written: 'Do not be afraid, daughter of Zion. Look, your king is coming, sitting on a donkey's colt!' His disciples did not understand these things at first; but when Jesus was glorified, then they remembered that these things had been written of him and had been done to him.
>(Jn 12:12-16)

Reflection

This scripture passage is proclaimed as the gospel at the blessing of the palms. It is a gospel of Jesus' triumph and of Jesus' humility. As a gospel of triumph it records the high point in Jesus' acceptance by his people. The teeming crowd, the mass of poor people, make his entry into the Holy City a triumphal entry. They shout their hosannas; they bless the one 'who comes in the name of the Lord' and call him 'the King of Israel!' They bow their palm fronds in deference before him. They are true Israelites, for all their poverty, and they know their scriptures. The greetings they shout at Jesus are all greetings of praise from Ps 118, a psalm entitled 'A Hymn of Thanksgiving to the Saviour of Israel.' The crowds, at this moment, hail Jesus as Israel's Saviour even if, a few days later, they will not understand why the Saviour of Israel must end in suffering and death.

As a gospel of humility it shows us Israel's greatest son entering the city of God as its rightful king. He has more right than any Herod or Caesar to enter Jerusalem in glory. He is of David's house and lineage, the house and lineage of the Saviour of Israel. Yet, look at who and what are not present at his triumphal procession! Among the crowds that greet Jesus, there is no welcoming court of Herod. The Sanhedrin and the ruling parties are not there either. There is no guard of honour. In fact, no one who is anyone of importance is there! An emperor rides a stallion in his triumphal entry into a city: Jesus rides a lowly donkey. Triumphal streets are normally decked with garlands and flower petals donated by the rich: our Lord's way is lined by the poor with branches from the commonest tree of the wayside, the palm tree. The cloaks of the wealthy cushion the stallion's prancing feet: the homespun cloaks of the poor barely silence the donkey's unshod feet. In this estimate, the scene on Palm Sunday is a marvel of the Lord's humility.

But Jesus deliberately chooses a donkey to ride on. He intends this seemingly humiliating choice, not as a lesson in humility as such, but as a Messianic statement about himself. In choosing a donkey to ride on, he is realising the Messianic prophecy of Zechariah, 'Rejoice heartily, O daughter Zion; shout for joy, O daughter Jerusalem! See, your king shall come to you; a just Saviour is he, meek, and riding on a donkey.' (Zech 9:9)

Our scripture passage presents us with an insight into the Messiahship of Jesus as he understood the Messiahship. It is a spiritual and a saving Messiahship as opposed to an earthly and a political one. The core issue for him is the breaking of the rule of sin over the human heart and in society and its replacement by the rule or reign of God and grace. Jesus is the lowly Messiah, the beast of burden himself, who carries the weight of human sin to the absolution of the cross. Only after the cross can the eschatological dimension of his Messiahship take place. Then, Messiahship becomes God's glorious reign of justice, peace and love over those now-redeemed hearts and in their new society.

Prayer

Our Father: May the saving Messiahship of your beloved Son be vindicated in our hearts and in society. May we be full of faith and committed to the task of building the kingdom. May we encourage every effort in art and science, in education and technology which increases human well-being and see it as an auxiliary to the blossoming of the kingdom on earth. 'Thy kingdom come. Thy will be done on earth as it is in heaven.' Amen.

Activity for Holy Week

Attend as many of the liturgical ceremonies this week as work and home obligations permit.

Monday in Holy Week

Anointing For Burial

Scripture passage

Six days before the Passover Jesus came to Bethany, the home of Lazarus, whom he had raised from the dead. There they gave a dinner for him. Martha served, and Lazarus was one of those at table with him. Mary took a pound of costly perfume made of pure nard, anointed Jesus' feet, and wiped them with her hair. The house was filled with the fragrance of the perfume. But Judas Iscariot, one of his disciples (the one who was about to betray him), said, 'Why was this perfume not sold for three hundred denarii and the money given to the poor?' (He said this not because he cared about the poor, but because he was a thief; he kept the common purse and used to steal what was put into it.) Jesus said, 'Leave her alone. She bought it so that she might keep it for the day of my burial. You always have the poor with you, but you do not always have me.'
(Jn 12:1-8)

Reflection

In the gospel accounts of the last days of Jesus, there is confusion as to the identity of the woman who anoints Jesus before his death. In John's gospel – our scripture passage – the woman is Mary of Bethany, the sister of Martha and Lazarus. On the other hand, Luke's gospel gives the woman no name. In fact, he calls her a great sinner, and thus she is not likely to be Mary of Bethany. Mark does not give her a name either. And neither does Matthew. There may have been more than one anointing by more than one woman, or the gospel writers may be confused over the details of a single anointing.

The woman has 'a pound of costly perfume'. She pours the precious ointment on Jesus' feet in an act of anointing. It is, of course, also an act of love. It is counterpoint to the action of hate on the part of the high priests and the elders who are this moment plotting Jesus' death. It is also counterpoint to the act of betrayal by Judas which follows on from this scene.

Judas (in the other gospels, the disciples) is indignant over the woman's largesse with the ointment worth 'three hundred denarii', the equal of a year's wages for a working man. Judas' reaction to this 'waste' is the reaction of his tight heart and hard-nosed economics. It is not the reaction of the liberal economics of love. Love is by nature uneconomical. Love is by nature extravagant. Love is prodigal. Even when love has given all it has to give, says William Barclay, 'it still thinks the gift too little.' (*Daily Study Bible: Matthew*) Presciently, Jesus says that the woman has done what she has done for his burial.

Judas is blind to any reality or symbol expressed by the woman's anointing. He ignores the fact that the guest at a banquet is anointed. He knows that Jesus as 'the Anointed of God' is entitled to a more lavish anointing than that given to the high priests (who even now are plotting Jesus' death). And he knows that Jesus' life is under extreme threat if only from the fact that Jesus relates the woman's anointing to 'the day of my burial'. And Judas, with a little reflection, would have known that the Jewish authorities will likely try to prevent the anointing of the body of Jesus later when he dies as a 'blasphemer'. Jesus is allowing his body to receive its anointing now from the woman in anticipation of its burial.

Prayer

Lord Jesus: May I learn from the woman who anointed you so lavishly. May my love for you be likewise lavish. May it be extravagant. May it be extreme. And when you answer my prayer and give me the intense love for you for which I pray, and for which I have long prayed, may I give all this intense love to you and think my gift too little. Amen.

Tuesday in Holy Week

Following Him

Scripture passage

Simon Peter said to him, 'Lord, where are you going?' Jesus
answered, 'Where I am going, you cannot follow me now;
but you will follow afterwards.' Peter said to him, 'Lord, why
can I not follow you now? I will lay down my life for you.'
Jesus answered, 'Will you lay down your life for me? Very
truly, I tell you, before the cock crows, you will have denied
me three times.'

(Jn 13:36-38)

Reflection

Peter asks, 'Lord, where are you going?' Where the Lord is
going is Calvary, and the awful humiliation and suffering which
precede it. Jesus looks at Peter and says, 'Where I am going, you
cannot follow me now.' We must not read this as a slighting of
Peter. Jesus loves him, and dearly. But he knows him inside out
and so he knows that Peter is not ready for what someone has
called 'the red road of martyrdom'. Peter is, in fact, so unready
that Jesus must tell him, 'Before the cock crows [i.e. before dawn
breaks] you will have denied me three times.'

The Peter we see in the gospels is the Peter who is not ready.
The Peter we see later in the Acts of the Apostles is the Peter
who is ready. Peter of the gospels is a man of huge but untrained
and impulsive heart. Peter of the Acts of the Apostles is a man of
huge and examined heart. It is of this later Peter that Jesus says,
'Where I am going ... you will follow afterwards.'

Anyone reading the gospel scenes involving Peter must find
great comfort in the man. He is of great heart, always the first to
promise but, like ourselves, often failing to fulfil. His weaknesses
are surely the pattern of our own. So often he is boastful but
empty; righteously angry and wrongly incensed; ready to take
on the whole world for Christ but then flinching at the last moment, even denying the Lord he manifestly loves so much.

What did Jesus see in him? He called him as the first apostle. He included him in special moments (such as the transfiguration) when nearly all the others were excluded. He made him the rock on which the faith of the disciples would rest in the troubled days after Jesus' death, yet had to admonish him three times to care for them. He knew that Peter would embarrass him in his agony, cutting off the ear of the high priest's servant and then denying his Lord three times, and all in the same night and despite three years of learning in the Lord's company! So what did Jesus see in him? He must have seen a huge heart and great potential. Here was a man who learned everything the hard way. But isn't that the sure and the enduring way? And perhaps Jesus saw in the man who 'wept bitterly' over his weakness the enduring love to which the flock and the good news of the kingdom of God could be safely committed. So he said to Peter: 'I have prayed that your faith not fail; and once you have turned back, you must strengthen your brothers.' (Lk 22:32)

Prayer

Dearest Jesus: I see so much of Peter in myself and in my grand promises but weak performances for the blessing of your name! It is the earlier Peter I am with my weaknesses, denials and sin. Please grant me a measure of the later Peter. Kindly grant me the gift of the tears that came from the deepest part of this great-hearted man. And continue to allow me, unworthy though I am, the charge of serving the faith of my sisters and brothers in any way that is open to me in ministry, prayer and love. Amen.

Wednesday in Holy Week

Never Despairing

Scripture passage

When it was evening, he took his place with the twelve; and
while they were eating, he said, 'Truly I tell you, one of you
will betray me.' And they became greatly distressed and
began to say to him one after another, 'Surely not I, Lord?' He
answered, 'The one who has dipped his hand into the bowl
with me will betray me. The Son of Man goes as it is written
of him, but woe to that one by whom the Son of Man is betrayed! It would have been better for that one not to have
been born.' Judas, who betrayed him, said, 'Surely not I,
Rabbi?' He replied, 'You have said so.'
(Mt 26:20-25)

Reflection

Judas decided on betraying Jesus for thirty pieces of silver. Some
scripture scholars wonder about the betrayal. Was Judas moti-
vated by avarice? The apostle John insists he was. But a mere
thirty pieces of silver isn't all that much then or now. Or did
Judas act out of spite because he was a revolutionary and became disillusioned with Jesus and his turn-the-other-cheek theology? Or was his betrayal not intended to end in Jesus' death at
all but to serve as the catalyst which would spur Jesus and 'the
company' about him into action against the Romans and so establish the new kingdom and the new social order? Did Judas
really intend to betray Jesus, or did something go horribly wrong?
One doesn't wish to be revisionist, merely to sift through possible motives and find the fatal flaw in this most condemned man
in Christian history.

We haven't the time for all of that here. The Christian record
of the passion and death of Jesus (as gathered in the gospels)
bends us to the belief that Judas intended his betrayal, and knew
its consequences for Jesus. He acted in cold blood, out of avarice,
and because, as John puts it simply, 'Satan entered into him.'

(Jn 13:27) The gospel accounts allow no room for excuses. In John's account of Jesus' prayer for his disciples at the Last Supper, Jesus says, 'Holy Father ... I protected them in your name that you have given me. I guarded them, and not one of them was lost except the one destined to be lost, so that the scripture might be fulfilled.' (Jn 17:12) The one 'destined to be lost' is Judas.

Awful as Judas' betrayal of Jesus was, it was not his greatest sin. His greatest sin was in not seeking forgiveness. While Matthew's gospel says that Judas 'repented' (Mt 27:3), the repentance was misdirected or lacking because Matthew immediately writes one of the most forlorn lines in scripture: 'Throwing down the pieces of silver in the temple, [Judas] departed; and he went and hanged himself.' (Mt 27:5) Judas despaired to the extreme of taking his own life in preference to forgiveness. It is through this sin, rather than in his betrayal, that he turned his back on Jesus and rejected the redemptive theology of the passion and death of the Lord in his own regard.

Prayer

Lord Jesus: Mine was a generation schooled to understand denial and betrayal mostly in terms of institutions and not sufficiently in terms of individuals. Loyalty to the church, to the state, to the cause, to the institution was the by-word we were taught. Were we too loyal to our institutions, loving them in our huge youthful idealism and with our so generous and so unexamined love? Did they deserve all we gave them? And were you, and 'the little ones' of the flock and of our daily lives, shortchanged in the process? Forgive us whatever must be forgiven in this history. Yet do not allow the generations that follow us to deny the institutions that serve them. They have been chastened and remain capable of much good. However, may they be generations that put you at the centre of their idealism and of their love, with all 'the little ones' of this world and of their lives firmly attached to you. Amen.

Holy Thursday

Service Always

Scripture passage

> Jesus got up from the table, took off his outer robe, and tied a
> towel around himself. Then he poured water into a basin and
> began to wash the disciples' feet and to wipe them with the
> towel that was tied around him ... After he had washed their
> feet, had put on his robe, and had returned to the table, he
> said to them, 'Do you know what I have done to you? You
> call me Teacher and Lord – and you are right, for that is what
> I am. So if I, your Lord and Teacher, have washed your feet,
> you also ought to wash one another's feet. For I have set you
> an example, that you also should do as I have done to you.'
> (Jn 13:4-15)

Reflection

In our scripture passage, Jesus is having his farewell supper
with his friends. On the religious level, he is celebrating
Passover with his disciples, and he is about to institute the mom-
entous ritual that we call the Mass. On the personal level, he is
about to pass from this world to the Father. At this critical time,
when he should be absorbed with these matters, what does he
do? He starts washing feet!

Washing feet has no apparent relationship with what has
been unfolding thus far in the Passover meal and the farewell
supper. It comes as something entirely unexpected. But, obviously, Jesus knew what he was doing. He intended this unusual
incident, and he intended it to underline a fundamental
Christian teaching. It is this: service is our most important product. Service is the practical expression of the commandment of
love. A Christian is defined by service.

Our Lord teaches by doing. It is he alone who picks up the
basin, pours water into it, bends down each time as he passes
from one disciple to the next. He does the washing, he does the
drying. There is no pious sermon here. Our Lord's actions are

his words. When he finishes he asks, 'Do you know (i.e. understand) what I have done to you? You call me Teacher and Lord –
and you are right, for that is what I am. So if I, your Lord and
Teacher, have washed your feet, you also ought to wash one another's feet. For I have set you an example, that you also should
do as I have done to you.' If we do not understand the centrality
of loving service in the life of the Christian then 'you will have
no inheritance with me.' (Jn 13:8)

Our own lives, to the contrary, are full of scrambling for
recognition and for the position and the status that require others to serve us. We are miffed when others do not give us the
deference due our titles, or the place of honour our dignity as-
sumes it deserves. William Barclay writes that here in this scripture passage is 'the lesson that there is only one kind of greatness, the greatness of service. The world is full of people who are
standing on their dignity when they ought to be kneeling at the
feet of their brethren.' (*Daily Study Bible: John*)

Let us not hear these words, nod our heads in pious agree-
ment, and say, 'What a lovely thought!' Let us believe the lovely
thought in the way Jesus believed it – by doing it – as he, our
Lord and Master, did as an example for us.

Prayer
Lord Jesus: The church is nothing and I am nothing without
love. Impress on me this truth which you taught as you washed
the feet of your apostles. Love is active. Love is dynamic. Love is
always 'in service' of others. May I live the Little Flower's insight: 'I saw that love alone moved the church, and that were
this love to fail, apostles would no longer spread the gospel, and
martyrs would refuse to shed their blood. I saw that all voc-
ations are summed up in love.' (*Autobiography*) May the love of
always trying to serve you and your brothers and sisters be
mine. Amen.

Good Friday

Were You There?

Scripture passage

It was now about noon, and darkness came over the whole land until three in the afternoon, while the sun's light failed; and the curtain of the temple was torn in two. Then Jesus, crying with a loud voice, said, 'Father, into your hands I commend my spirit.' Having said this, he breathed his last. When the centurion saw what had taken place, he praised God and said, 'Certainly, this man was innocent.' And when all the crowds who had gathered there for this spectacle saw what had taken place, they returned home, beating their breasts. But all his acquaintances, including the women who had followed him from Galilee, stood at a distance, watching these things.

(Lk 23:44-49)

Reflection

The novels and stories we read reflect human life and the human condition. That is their attraction for us. We find ourselves in the characters of these novels and stories and in the situations they find themselves in. We also find ourselves in the characters portrayed in the scriptures and in the situations they found themselves in. And so, we find ourselves in one or other of the characters that make up the great drama of Good Friday.

What part do we play in this tragedy that is the passion and death of Jesus? We say, excusing ourselves, that we weren't there, that it all happened two thousand years ago. But Calvary happens every day in some form. It is repeated every day in some faraway dictatorship and in our own society at home; in some vast city and in our small rural community; in drug-infested families and in the family of which we are a member. We may say, correctly, that we weren't at the original Calvary and played no part in the historical suffering and death of Jesus, but we cannot say that Calvary does not repeat itself in one form or another in every generation, including our own, and we cannot avoid playing a part in its modern versions.

What part do I play in the drama? Am I Peter, denying my faith in the office or in the pub because I lack backbone? Am I Pilate, washing my hands of a decision that calls for justice because I'm afraid to upset the higher-ups in the company and in the church? Am I the fickle mob that shouts, 'Away with him! Away with him!' when some half-way house tries to locate on my street? Am I the culturally conditioned soldier who mocks and taunts the foreign worker under the cross of his or her agony? Am I the cowardly disciples who flee when the going gets rough with people of colour coming into the neighbourhood?

Or, am I the weeping women of Jerusalem who can empathise with a victim because I have a nurturing heart? Am I the Veronica of legend who has the guts to do something and, because of which, I find an impression of Jesus and a grace left on my soul? Am I Simon of Cyrene, no hero and not sure what the politics of the situation calls for, but I let goodness get the better of me? Am I Joseph of Arimathea who risks my social and religious position because my heart is human? Am I Mary, the mother, who picks up the pieces of a life destroyed by the blindness and the bigotry of others? When I see today's version of the Victim of Calvary, do my eyes pass over his and her head as though he and she were not there, or do my eyes meet theirs, and answer their pain?

Were you there when they crucified my Lord? asks the touching hymn of that title. In terms of historical time, the answer is No, I was not there. But, in another sense, the answer is Yes, I am there. For the scandal of Calvary is a blight that is still with us. Only the most insensitive person fails to realise that Calvary and its Victim and its cast of characters did not appear just once in history, and that a long, long time ago.

Prayer

Dearest Jesus: You were the victim of the blindness of your enemies and the sins of your friends. I would wither away in shame for my part in this tragedy had you not said that you were laying down your life freely and for love of me. I'll never understand the mystery of such love, but I'll never tire of thanking you for it. In the cross is your love and my salvation. Amen.

Holy Saturday

Seeing Deeper Than Sight

Scripture passage

> When evening had come, and since it was the day of Preparation, that is, the day before the sabbath, Joseph of Arimathea, a respected member of the council, who was also himself waiting expectantly for the kingdom of God, went boldly to Pilate and asked for the body of Jesus. Then Pilate wondered if he were already dead; and summoning the centurion, he asked him whether he had been dead for some time. When he learned from the centurion that he was dead, he granted the body to Joseph. Then Joseph bought a linen cloth, and taking down the body, wrapped it in the linen cloth, and laid it in a tomb that had been hewn out of the rock. He then rolled a stone against the door of the tomb. Mary Magdalene and Mary the mother of Joses saw where the body was laid.
>
> (Mk 15:42-47)

Reflection

Jesus chose the apostles to be the witnesses of his life and ministry which culminated in his death and burial. Such witness, he knew, would be necessary for the historical record and to future generations of his followers. All had to be completed according to the Father's will and show Jesus' love is poured out for us to the last drop. It is striking, then, that the apostles have long since fled the scene and that the 'women who followed him' all the way from Galilee are the witnesses to his death and burial. 'The chosen male disciples have abandoned Jesus,' writes Wilfrid Harrington. 'These women disciples have stood steadfast and have not been ashamed of Jesus.' (*New Testament Message: Mark*) Women today celebrate this fact and accuse churchmen of making too little of it in the context of ordained ministry. Leaving that issue aside for the moment, we may say that the women who followed Jesus to the bitter end were surely the ones who loved him unconditionally.

The synoptic gospel writers stress the fact that the faithful women 'witnessed' or 'watched' or 'saw' the death on Calvary and the burial. Mark says that they 'saw where the body was laid' as though inferring that they took unusual notice. Matthew says they 'watched everything,' inferring the same intensity of notice. Luke says they 'saw the tomb and how the body was laid in it' as though noting facts or details that would serve a future purpose. The spiritual writer Anselm Grün tells us that the Greek verb which Luke uses can mean that the women saw both physically and with spiritual insight, that they 'saw' that this was not an end but a preparation, a preparation of the tomb for the resurrection in which Jesus would rise 'into the clarity of God.' (*Jesus: The Image of Humanity*)

Prayer
Lord Jesus: Help me to see as the faithful women saw. Help me to see you beyond death and tomb in your resurrection and in glory. Help me to see my own future in your present. Help me then to live my life, and form my values, from this perspective of eternity. And may I see all people in the light of your loving eyes, and value them as you valued them with the shedding of your most precious blood. And may I say of you and your tomb: 'O Christ! You slept a life-giving sleep in the grave and awoke humankind from the heavy sleep of sin.' (*Orthodox Liturgy: Holy Saturday*) Thank you now and forever. Amen.